Escaping the
Dark Shadow

Escaping the Dark Shadow

Published by The Conrad Press Ltd. in the United
Kingdom 2023

Tel: +44(0)1227 472 874
www.theconradpress.com
info@theconradpress.com

ISBN 978-1-915494-76-4

Typesetting and cover design by:
Michelle Emerson, michelleemerson.co.uk
Cover photograph taken by Keith Perkins.

The Conrad Press logo was designed by Maria Priestley.

Printed and bound in Great Britain by Clays Ltd,
Elcograf S.p.A.

Escaping the Dark Shadow

Keith Perkins

Contents

Author's Note

This is my true story beginning at the age of four years old. I am sure there are many people especially around my age group, who were not blatantly or even knowingly abused, but Parents were losing control of the new war. liberation, and the start of a battle between the old and young of every generation.

I can only liken it to a dark shadow trying to destroy the enlightenment of true liberation, for everyone in our generation and those to come. Hence the title of this book. ·

For me, an incident triggered a chain of events, which meant I would never have a 'normal' life, whatever defines this. Subtle abuse builds, but whilst destructive, those who have faced it and found their own ways of controlling it, can turn the energy into positivity. Even so the transformation from victim can be slow and difficult with, the line between sanity and insanity a fine one.

To define the period starting with the sudden transformation in my body and mind. I include Brief accounts of significant modern historical events during my life to date.

Hopefully with the much lighter and humorous side of life from school, work, marriage, parenthood and into old age. Finally, I include my understanding of the methods used by the governments of the so-called free world to control us. To date, where the incompetent minority, having not one but three chances of voting to put our country into the hands of a competent leader. Eventually all ending in failure.

Keith Perkins
July 2023

Preface

I was born at the end of the reign, and life, of George VI. One year after my birth our country was under the rule of Queen Elizabeth II. She was to live as the Queen of the United Kingdom for the largest part of my life. And now I'm living under the reign of King Charles III.

In March 2022, I sent a drawing I'd done, of Her Majesty the Queen and her son the Prince of Wales's wife the Duchess of Cornwall, to the Queen herself. As the Prince of Wales was divorced, just like the Duchess, society's complete acceptance of them surely shows a remarkable breaking with tradition and the old values.

I was surprised to get a positive response from the palace. It said that Her Majesty the Queen was pleased to hear from me and greatly appreciated the sketch I'd sent her. This pleasant and courteous reply from Her Majesty the Queen, a remarkable lady born into great privilege and who served our nation so magnificently during her long reign, led me to think about my own childhood and how I had been controlled and treated without courtesy most of the time.

Also, due to the enormous change in society's attitudes towards all manner of fundamental things (in the not-so-distant past, Prince Charles's divorce and his wife's divorce would unquestionably have barred them from becoming king and queen), I was inspired to write about the many, changes in society throughout my life. And at a personal level, there have been so many instances of people being given control over people, especially young people, and how they abused that power and revealed their own motivations over the vulnerable people under their control, to be utterly appalling and absolutely selfish.

I also noted that I had lived through times of liberation, only to be taken full circle back to the control and abuse of the vulnerable, in every country in the world.

This control and abuse has often been practised under the much-publicised guise of saving the planet. Arguably even the widespread social response to Covid has been part of a programme to control and restrict our way of life.

How much greed and self-interest politicians themselves practise is extraordinary, whether in the House of Commons itself or in TV reality shows set in remote places.

Many more are driven by self-importance and greed. Back just before I was born, a certain individual was beginning his political career, 1949 London County council, election. Then in February 1959 the same person, a certain John Stonehouse, travelled to Rhodesia and Nyasaland on a fact-finding mission, where he encouraged the oppressed Black people, to stand up for their rights and stated that the Labour party supported their cause.

He was very quickly deported from Southern Rhodesia and banned from returning. Stonehouse negotiated an agreement for technological co-operation between the Czech Republic and Britain. This eventually led to the alleged control and manipulation of him by the Czechoslovak secret service. Much more information can be found on the internet, but eventually he faked his own death. He then went ahead to transfer money between banks, until he was spotted by a bank teller. Eventually he was arrested but unbelievably, released on bail to continue to serve as an MP. He ended up making a fortune in writing, TV appearances and radio broadcasts.

My own existence is boring compared to the many colourful characters that have graced our political parties and media, and I doubt Unique.

However, I often wonder how many more people are like me? When I read books or watch films, the writers, or producers, in many cases could have been basing the story line in the book or film, loosely on my life so far, and maybe even into my future.

My recollection of the beginning of my life started long ago in an old council house, known back then, as two up two down. It had an outside toilet at the end of a narrow garden. The house was situated in a rough area by reputation.

I start my clear memory of events at the age of four years, I do remember things before that, but not as vivid as the years in this story. May 1955, so what can you say about a life that began simple and straight forward, but where nothing is what it seems, much like the present.

Chapter 1

Unique or not unique that is the question?

My new sister, she's here, I am so excited, I know there is a bottle of special drink to celebrate, my dad said we will drink it when she arrives, I will give them a surprise, get it, and take it to them, this will make him happy he may give me a hug.

I remember thinking this is very heavy, I can't hold it, its slipping. No please don't smash. The sound of breaking glass echoed through the house, it sounded to me, like a truck had driven through the wall.

I could hear him coming where can I go, he knows where I hide, but under the table no one can see me, when I am under the table, I become invisible. He's coming closer I'll close my eyes and disappear. It is quiet now everything has gone I am alone, in my darkness, the bottle is whole again and we will all be happy he will pick me up and take me to see my new sister.

The peacefulness has been broken, and I am being pulled from the darkness, the feeling is back I feel sick, and I can't breathe. No dad please don't hit me the bottle jumped out of my hand, I only wanted to make you happy, please, please. I saw his hand rise and I bathed myself in the blackness that always protected me, this time mum wasn't there to stop him, so I had to hold on to the darkness for longer, I knew if I could make the water in my eye's he might stop, but sometimes it makes it worse he calls me a baby and hits me harder.

I remember once I had a thing my mum called a dummy, I loved it, it was my friend, when I felt sad or lonely, even when I was tired it made me feel safe. One day he broke it, he laughed and said it was time I grew up, but my mother made him buy me a new one, but it wasn't my friend, I didn't feel the same. I needed my friend, somehow it would have taken away the pain, it always worked.

After a while he told me that he forgave me putting the blame on me rather than on him and told me that he only smacked me to teach me right from wrong and to be strong.

Although I was only four years old a voice in my head told me that I didn't break the bottle on purpose I wanted to be kind and show them all, that I was pleased to have a new sister, was that right or wrong? The smacking just made him feel good, a substitute instead of drinking the wine. I just wanted him for once to hold me and tell me it didn't matter, my sister was the happy event, and she was waiting to see me, instead he told me that I couldn't see her in case I broke her too.

I was lucky because I had a new friend, a voice that came into my darkness and told me what to do when I was afraid or in pain, little did I know I would meet this friend, who would be the most terrifying apparition that set me on a path that I would never really come to terms with or understand.

So, finally the day came when I had to go to a place they called school, I already knew this was a building inside green railings, just across the road from where I lived. I had to dress up in what my mum called a uniform, but it wasn't like a soldier or a bus conductor, it was just posh shorts and a jumper over a little tie.

There were bigger boys and girls at this school and the bigger boys pushed you over and tried to make you cry. I remember a little boy in my class always crying because he was picked on. I could not understand why, he was nice to me and used to talk about cars and toys he had, but he always looked sad. Then it happened to me.

I was sitting on the wall when a big boy came up to me and asked if I had any toy cars, I said I did, and he asked me to bring some in to show him, but not tell the teachers as this was just our secret. I was pleased that a big boy wanted to be my friend.

That evening, I picked out two of my toy cars and hid them in my lunch box. When I showed him them at lunch, he took them and told me to bring more, or he would beat me up. I didn't know what to do, this had never happened before now I knew what my little friend must have felt. So, I decided I would take in some more of my cars hoping that I would be safe from bullying, but after a couple more times I was running out of cars to take into the school.

I never realised that my mum could see what was happening and had told my father that she thought I was being bullied at school. I was sitting at the table with my breakfast when my father grabbed me by my jumper and threw me onto a chair, 'where are your cars?' He demanded, 'at school I replied',' don't lie to me' he said and raised his hand to hit me. I flinched in a gesture to protect myself, 'the big boy took them from me' I said, trying to force some tears into my eyes to get his sympathy, I don't know why because that had never worked up to now.

'As big as me?' he said, I said nothing in reply, although I felt a happy feeling, that at last he was going to protect me and make this big boy give me all my toy cars back.

Wrong again, he put his face close to me and said, 'if they are not back here tonight, I will give you a good hiding, you pathetic little coward.'

Only I knew that my friend visited me that night, he was great, I still did not know what he looked like, but he always made me feel sure that whatever he told me to do always worked. He continued, 'always be the first, never wait remember, if they are bigger than you, kick them between the legs,'. I did not know why, but I knew it was a sensitive area, because I once had a football hit me there and I was in pain for quite a long time.

I went off to school the next morning and all I could think about was break time and in my head rehearsed the action to make sure I would hit the target first time.

So, break time came, and the big boy met me at the same place as usual, 'so where`s my car' he said, I looked him in the eyes, stood back slightly, then kicked as hard as I could.

His face turned first into a look of shock and disbelief, then as he hit the ground, he screamed out in shear agony, the voice from the darkness told me to kick him hard so that he didn`t get up, the blackness surrounded me, and the voice took over until I was raised into the air by a teacher and told in a loud voice to stop.

The darkness floated away; the bully huddled in a tight ball screaming and the other big boy`s stared in disbelief.

I was taken to the headmistress, and I told her my story, of course, I didn`t tell her my father had told me to do it. From that day I ended up with more cars than I had ever given to the bully and the big boys stayed away from me.

This was not that good because nobody could relax with me. I began however to understand the darkness, it protected me, all I had to do was to give my thoughts to its control and the rest just happened.

Even after bringing back all my toy cars and more besides, nothing was ever said on the outcome between me and my father and nothing happened to improve my father's relationship with me. There was nothing I could do to please him, and I came to detest him.

I had just left the school to go to the junior school, where the pupils were even bigger, and I had another sister appear, luckily there were no bottles of wine to break, but while we were out at my grandparents to sleep overnight, the metal was taken from the roof of our house and the rainwater flooded the inside.

The area was quite renowned for being a rough area and there was a traveller's camp close by, so these types of incidents were common. I got on with them, although my father threatened me what would happen if he caught me playing with them, he thought they were all uneducated but a few of them were at our school, and some were cleverer than most of the other boys.

The house itself was a mid-terraced, with a toilet outside the back door, it was cold and damp, so you did not want to hang around in there, the seat was always freezing in the winter even though it was made of wood. The strange thing was, it was better than the one at my nans house, that's my dads' mother. Theirs was at the end of the long garden and was just a wooden bench with a hole in it, and under was a large bucket, a man with a horse and cart used to come every two or three days and empty the buckets from their toilet and the persons next door. He was an exceptionally large man and even he struggled to carry them both together, one in each hand.

Chapter 2

Manure, manure, everywhere

There are a few things that I will never forget for as long as I live. The first is the day that we had a fall of snow, and the ground was very slippery. Back then my grandmother used to sprinkle salt from a big container over the snow and ice, this she told me was to melt the snow. It always seemed strange because it worked, but because she was up at six in the morning to get breakfast for my grandad and uncles before they left for work. She salted the path for them so they could do their daily business in the toilet. But by eight o`clock it had re-frozen.

The big man arrived at around eight thirty, you could hear the clip clop of the horses' hooves on the road and the sound of children's voices, our job was to follow the horse with a bucket and collect its droppings for the garden. I did not understand about organics until much later, so I thought, why didn't my nan just get the man to empty our waste on the garden and save me following a horse carrying tons of shit with the sole purpose of collecting, its shit? Having to fight with the other kids on the same pointless mission.

As he came down the path with the two buckets, the now re-frozen melted snow under the newly formed white covering, lay in wait to capture any unsuspecting pray, the perfect snare. Over he went, his arms incapable of acting as balancers, as he dropped both buckets and fell, all three objects hit the ground together, he of course slid further down the path than the two buckets, which hit the ground simultaneously throwing their entire contents down on him from headfirst to his feet. It looked like a brown murky tidal wave covering a rock formation. Fear was the only thing that discouraged me from bursting into laughter.

Everyone came rushing out of the immediate houses, including my nan. He was washed down with a hosepipe, given some old overalls to change into and some brandy to alleviate the possibility of catching some type of disease. The total washdown and clean up time, including the sanitisation of the pathway, using enough disinfection to cause your eyes to water if you got within six feet of the disaster area. Was over an hour.

This was an all-round success, as all us kids were concerned, as we got to fill our seaside buckets, good old Neddie had eaten half a bale of hay and produced enough manure to top up all the compositors in the immediate area.

Getting back to the saga of our house in Chatham. The house was owned by the Council, and they were obliged to re-home us as they decided to demolish the whole row of houses, so eventually we were moved to a new house on a council estate, but it was a long way from our house and my school. It was not an immediate move as nothing ever is where government departments are concerned. So in between the loss of our house and the move, we were housed in a couple of the rooms above one of the local shop. It was only for a short while, but the grocer and his wife were good to us, and my father was unusually kind to us all, including me.

Maybe because of the diversion and disruption to normality the darkness did not appear during the period at the shop, which felt strange, I began to think it may have lived in the old house and decided to stay there after we left, a stupid idea, but I missed the feeling of self-assurance it gave me, when it was in me. I thought I was invincible.

I wished that it would return, I felt secure when it was with me, like nothing could ever harm me, little did I know that a far sinister darkness lurked within the void left behind, a more adult version, not as friendly and comforting, in fact it was terrifying, yet at the same time exciting. It brought an inexplainable and sometimes uncontrollable power into my life.

This was a power that proved to shape the rest of my life, in many ways, some good and some frightening.

We eventually moved to a new house, it had three bedrooms and best of all a toilet inside the house, no more freezing at the bottom of the garden and running in the rain bursting for a wee, because you had left it too long.

I had a bedroom of my own, admittedly it was small, but I could close the door and be alone. This was to begin the real start of my strange life, but nevertheless a fantastic one in many ways. I know as you read on, you will think it is a fictional story, or at the very least exaggerated to a great extent, and I must admit sometimes, some of the things I write about, do not seem impossible even to me. I am pleased to say, at least I have witnesses and evidence that many of the incidences did in fact happen as I have recounted them.

As I mentioned before, we now had a new sister in our family, at first it felt strange to have someone else that had to be considered, when we were running around making a noise. I didn`t know then or to this day why, but she was special to me, I sensed a strange kind of bond between us from her birth, one I never felt with my first sister.

Little did I know this would change dramatically during our lives, although never was there a definitive reason, other than the way I treated her. My elder sister was there at the very start of the strange beginning of my conscious life, and I expected her to sense the same feelings as me. This was of course wrong to expect.

Because I always wanted to protect my younger sister, from my darker side, I drove a wedge between us, thinking that this would protect her, as I didn't even understand what was happening myself. Just that I needed to dominate to compensate for my own cowardly fears. We never had or made the opportunity to discuss all that went on in our early life together, the problems with our father and his effect on me, but then she was far too young to even understand the emotions that drove my actions and reactions. How could she when I was in the same position, trying to understand how I could change things into what? I didn't even know what was normal family life.

The same for my first sister Lynda, who I also loved and would have done anything to protect her, but I guess the experience with the wine bottle, and the scar of the incident at the table, remained in my subconscious mind, along with the comments of my father that she was watching me. His way of hinting that she was part of the reason I suffered the pain of my Fathers wrath, the classic tact of a bully.

It seems crazy when you become mature in later life, the things that you believed, and how gullible you were. Most of the children who are abused allow it because it begins so subtly, there is no clear starting point, it just develops, like a natural progression of life, but it is actively planned and orchestrated to achieve an end point of ultimate control.

It is just a personal level of dictatorship, the dictator craves adoration at first from people close to them, but then they crave more, which leads to embracing people outside of their adoring subjects and then no amount is enough.

Finally, the person or people outside of their circle become nothing to the dictator, but still they crave more praise or recognition, so a small, controlled amount of recognition is given in return. Just enough to make the subjects grateful and make them think they can get more by being even more adoring and most of all obedient.

It does not have to be just a craving to be loved, it can be a craving to be recognised, understood, respected for a talent or achievement that they never really had. But as the dictator or abuser loves and adores only themselves, nothing but themselves matter. This means the abused never really achieve any self-worth and will live with the oppression, sometimes becoming a mini- abuser themselves. It can only ever end, at any level, when the abused control their fear. You can never conquer fear, the best you can do is to bury it so deep inside it is rarely triggered.

The good or terrible thing in my case was, I never blamed myself for the actions, only for being too weak to stop them. Until that moment when I lost all fear because I had faced and defied the ultimate fear for many people, death itself.

I am pleased to say, I found an opportunity to discuss just a ridiculously small part of the reasons that we never were close, with Lynda and it did bring us a little closer together.

The truth was that I was never loved by my father, he resented the way my mother always gave me a lot of attention when there were just the three of us, four years is a brief time in an adult life.

I was told, in later life by aunts and uncles, that as a baby, my mother even held my hand and laid next to me to get me to sleep, it was his sadistic way to get his revenge and make me feel an outcast. He certainly made it clear that my sisters could never do anything wrong.

This had the desired effect, along with his words 'Lynda is watching you, so do not think you are safe. 'Now, after many years I know she was also afraid of him, and had suspicions about his character, not in the same way as I was in the beginning, but nevertheless afraid. An incident that remained with me for many years, back then seemed to re-enforce my thoughts about my older sister being used to further taunt and degrade me.

During dinner, we children, were arguing, my father made a comment about making a noise at the table, my elder sister answered him back. He looked at me and asked me what I had said, 'nothing' I replied, he then repeated 'what did you say don't lie to me.' I repeated 'nothing', I stupidly expected my sister to own up as the culprit, even though she was four years younger than me, just a young child. But she just lowered her head.

He then stood up and slapped me hard across the face. The moment his hand contacted my face the darkness descended over me, I looked him in the eyes and a voice came from inside one that I could not stop, as I said the words, I felt such a hatred, I was so stupid, I had no defence at all, he could have floored me with one punch, but that did not even come into my head.

All that came out of my mouth was. 'That is the last time you ever hit me.' I left the table and went to my room. It was then I realised that there must be something protecting me, something within me that I should try to bring out and use the power it gave me to my advantage, but what was it? how did it get there? how will I recognise it? and most of all how will I be able to control it.?

Up until that moment my father had totally controlled my life, I was terrified to go against him, which allowed him to, as they would define it today, psychologically abuse me.

I was ashamed of the things I allowed him to make me do, what some of them were I will never be able to divulge to anyone directly, but through the media of writing it may reach others and help them to know that they are not isolated in their fear and are not to accept the blame of being too weak to break the cycle. It takes far more than voices in your head, or one outburst of strength, to overcome the psychological impact combined with pure physical trauma.

Why? I hear you say, well firstly, because you think nobody would believe, secondly, I personally could never admit, let alone understand why I allowed him to make me do those things.

Worst and most confusing of all, could I even be enjoying the humiliation? In some ways it gave me an unexpected power over others, the very same individuals who already gave him control over their actions. Did it perversely make me think I was equal to him? If you think about it the people surrounding a dictator, draw their power from that person and appear to be in control themselves, but crossing the dictator means destruction.

Whatever the theory of how a dictator survives, all this was made possible because of my one overpowering weakness. Fear of him, or fear of my own emotions?

Now I am older and wiser, the one thing I could never have even contemplated back then, was the desperate need, I had for him to understand and most of all love me. All these atrocities will remain, as you cannot erase the fear when you are touched and although you resist with all your thoughts, your body reacts, ignoring your attempts to resist you feel an excitement, which makes you want more. You want to know why you feel more of these new sensations buried in your young body. But after you are finished with, the door is closed, and you hear first the laughter and then the exaggerated noises, you bury all your emotions, I am pleased to say, the way he has been buried for many years now.

All of us have our innermost secrets but I can only ever give some idea of the lesser things he did, which will give you a little appreciation of the worst.

Up to this very day I cannot believe I allowed these things to happen and can never forgive myself for being such a weak child. It was amazing how he managed to fool people into trusting him, he even did things that looked like he wanted to evaluate his actions just to see the limits of people's naivety and stupidity.

He certainly already knew how pathetic I was, how I wish that I could have joined with the darkness that showed me the way, much earlier, he may then have died even earlier and saved a lot of people their grief and pain.

Firstly, I must give you this paragraph that is an accolade to the potential brilliance he had at his disposal, making it even more of a travesty the way he acted towards people.

Chapter 3

Dark deception

In my short lifetime from my birth to his death. His achievements were in those days amazing by any standard, but his greatest weaknesses and constant downfalls were gambling on horse and greyhound racing and women. His achievements, however, were equal to his stupidity at not being able to control these obsessions.

I was informed by my mother, that he began working as a labourer, delivering parcels to the factory, where she worked as a bookkeeper. Before she met him, she was confident and full of promise. Just after my birth he got a driving and delivery job with a brick manufacturing company.

This suited him totally, he was away long distances, which enabled him to stay away at nights, allowing him to conduct one of his favourite pastimes, women. I now know, just to prove his innocence, he would occasionally take me with him on the trip. I thought he enjoyed taking me and was proud sitting in the big cab, but even then, I was his stool pigeon.

From this job he then decided to get an easier one and moved to the BP refinery on the isle of Grain, in Kent as the position of storeman.

It was obviously a lot easier to move up in position in the early days, but even so he very quickly gained promotion from storeman to a shift chemist position, dealing with the quality control of oil samples and progressed further to laboratory work. His charismatic disposition even had him voted in as a union shop steward representative.

Even with all this he decided to take on a part time job at a grocery store, assembling and delivering orders sent into the shop, to local customers.

No this was not to give him extra income to give us all a better life, it was to fuel his gambling and other addictions, and to exercise his devious brain, just to show how superior he was to others around him.

Here is a very tame example of the fantastic mind that he had, to plan and execute an operation without the detection of the most obvious of clues left behind to purposely arouse suspicions. As I was now getting older, he decided that I would help him to prepare and deliver these boxes of food, to give me some pocket money, that was the ploy anyway.

I was happy at first because I was paid a whole one pound and thought he was helping me to get some pocket money, up until then I just got the odd two old pence for some broken biscuits on the way to school.

All I had to do was to make up the boxes from the orders of customers and print the names and addresses on the boxes, from a list that he had written down for me.

While I ended up doing all the work, he chatted up the women, everyone thought he was fantastic, 'What a wonderful dad you have' was one of the comments I detested the most, I used to reply, 'you should try living with him.' Then one day I realised why he got me the job, not out of love, not even to save him a few pence pocket money. No, to use me to further one of his schemes.

Quite a simple one as it turned out. They didn`t realise I was making up boxes of grocery`s that didn`t have real orders from customers, I just got a list from him, then he would get me to write on boxes' The mixture of real, (ones with orders) and fictious, (ones without) names and addresses.

One I remember as Ms Hore, 2 Bulls cottages (Ms whore two balls cottages). He laughed as he wrote it down the first time and I was so naive that I did not realise the significance, mind you obviously nobody else did, unless one of the women he was having a relationship with, was in on the fraud.

He had told me that if I were caught making up

boxes, he would have to punish me for being stupid, I knew what that meant. I was yet again his stool pigeon.

My mother knew what he was doing at the shop and was terrified. I was upset that she did not stop him from doing it and resented the fact that she wasn't strong enough to go against him, how two faced of me, I was doing his dirty work as well, why should she fear him any less than me.

I learnt many years later why. He had told her that he had organised it so that if the fraud were discovered, everyone would think it was me stealing the food and drinks and if she ever spoke out against him, I would be the one to suffer.

It was much later and by accident, that I found he had hidden drinks in the ceiling of the shop storeroom.

During a stock delivery, the men delivering the stock knocked a ceiling tile out of place. They had bent the tile holder and the tile would not go back into place. I told them not to worry I would get some pliers from the manager, and straighten the holder, then it would push back in place, they were incredibly pleased.

When they had finished stacking the delivery boxes on the shelves, I brought in the manager, Mr Triggs, I got on well with him I do not flatter myself it was me, more than likely he thought my father was wonderful. He offered to get the panel back in place but as he was shorter than me, and round, I told him that I would do it. He was incredibly pleased, and it turned out for me, to be the best act of kindness I could have done.

As I tried to straighten up the recess the second tile dropped out and down came, a can of beer, chocolate bars and crisp packets. I quickly realised that this was my father's insurance policy, almost discovered by a clumsy delivery man.

This was the room that I used to pack the delivery boxes, the perfect place for his backup story should he be found with the falsely marked boxes, this time his luck had run out and mine had saved my embarrassment, as well as giving me one over on the bastard.

Just to re-enforce my superiority in this game of wits, I slipped them on to the van in the top of a falsely marked box without his knowledge, one I knew I would be dropping off at our house later in the round.

He was, as I must admit a very clever person although inspired by pure evil, later to become his undoing and allowing me to have my final revenge, sending him to his death in torment, far better than a sentence for murdering him.

So, what happened next? Well as far as he was concerned nothing had changed, so we continued as usual, I was waiting for him to make a mistake and point the finger at me, that would have been fantastic. Can you imagine his face when after constructing some explanation as to why he suspected me of hiding contraband, and then how he discovered where I had hidden it? Followed by why he had not tried to stop me? Presumably using the old cliché, he did not know what to do as I had always been a problem child. Poor old Earnie.

All these mind searching explanations, only to find an empty void in the exact place that the Manager had seen the tile fall out. I could not wait, I would have to be patient though, as I was learning the subtle art of manipulation of a dictator.

Knowing the end game, you can control a strategy from start to completion. The bastard is so vain he (or she) thinks they are in control, when the truth is they are so predictable, the simplest of minds can predict their next move. The only art is to predict when the next move is due.

At the end of my story, we see the same strategy employed by all the governments and leaders, of what we knew during my young life as 'the democratic free world,' soon to become the co-allision of arseholes.

Reduce the choices of parties, discredit the most popular small political parties, by encouraging the lead figures of those parties to appear as raving lunatics, they even allowed a party to register those very words. Understanding manipulation and control of a simple situation, means the complete understanding of the people involved in the situation, anticipation of their goals, and their underlying aim.

If I could understand my father, it would then be simple, but it was not, his greatest protection was his random actions, making it almost impossible to read any clear end goal, other than one of greed and self-indulgence, almost 90% of all the world's leaders, governments, and industrialists. I apologise to all those that don't fit the bill, I doubt few enough to.

Back to reality, I waited patiently for my chance to be in complete control of a situation, but unbelievably nobody saw through his scheme, eventually by chance rather than design by my hand, my final satisfaction would be complete sooner than I expected. For now, I had to be patient, strangely back then it was one of my assets.

During the delivery rounds we would go to our house, and he would get me to take in the boxes and hide the contraband in the cupboard under the stairs. Later to feature in his final days of life and be a source of final satisfaction to me.

Getting back to the main story, after my disappointment once again at being used as a tool without any thought of my feelings or worth. I continued with the deliveries, but with my newly found end game solution in place, I enjoyed delivering the boxes of groceries, when would we be found out?

I would of course, deliver most of them from the van to the door and he would deliver to the special customers, who needed particular care, all a certain kind, bed ridden by choice not because of illness.

It was during delivery the groceries that I learnt, my first unknown at that time, influence. I seemed to have had it then, and still have to this day.

Chapter 4

Albert the third

One of the customers I consistently delivered to, was an old woman who had a large German shepherd dog, she always enjoyed a chat with me and surprisingly my father encouraged me to have a good talk with her as it was 'good for customer relationships.' The dog used to be in the house when I delivered her box of groceries and would bark and leap at the inside of the door leading from the kitchen of the house to the garden, the whole of the time we were talking, not continuously but enough to re-enforce that it was there to ensure you did not get into the house. It in fact, gave the impression it wanted to get at you to tear you apart.

This day I got to the gate of the woman's house, but the dog was in the garden, not shut up in the kitchen. It raced up to the gate, barking and growling, as if the gate were a substitute for the kitchen door, but it could have easily cleared the gate with one leap. Strangely because of this I did not feel scared, it was all about boundaries.

As I did not want to take the chance of evaluating his insistence that behind any blockage stood for his domain. I did consider that I should go into the garden, in case the old lady had fallen but I finally decided to take the box back to the van. like a fool I thought my father would be worried about the old lady and come back with me to investigate.

When he was telling me his stories about how tough he was at the end of the World War Two. One of these stories was about how their regiment of the Scots Guards was sent to round up German soldiers and control German resistance in Berlin.

This meant special training, according to him. Part of this was to be trained on, if necessary, killing ex-Prisoner of war guard dogs. According to him a lot of the guards brought back their dogs and were using them as protection against the allied troops, checking on papers.

He told me many times about the day him and his best friend went to check on the papers of a senior German guard that they had found in a bar. When they got there this person had a large German Shepard dog with him. As they approached, he released the dog who leapt at my father, who according to him with one move killed the dog outright.

Because this story, obviously to keep me in awe of the power of my father and gave me the idea that he had no fear of any dog and would be able to go in the gate and check on the old lady. No such luck, I was told to take the box back or I would be given a 'kick up the arse, and that I was just a snivelling coward; the dog was just an excuse to be lazy.

This was just another situation that I had to deal with. I no longer felt fearful of him just pure contempt, I was still too young to physically stand up to him, but that would come, the problem was I could never be happy all the time he was there.

So I went back to the house, what could I do, his last advice to me was, 'Just go in the gate the dog is just unsure of you, be positive.' Words of wisdom or just an excuse to cover the bullshit that comes out of his mouth on regular basis.

I will never really know why I believed that voice in my head, which told me it would be ok, I just wanted to drop the box outside the gate and shout out, hoping the old woman came out to get it.

But I thought I needed to begin to listen to the voice in my head, so I took a deep breath and walked up to the gate, opened it as positively as I could, the dog, still snarling backed up a little.

I entered the garden then closed the gate behind me and began walking up the path, concentrating on the kitchen door, blotting out any fear I had in my head. The dog followed me and as I reached the kitchen door the old woman opened it.

She looked a little shocked, 'how did you get past Albert' she said. I just replied, 'he let me in, he knows me, he could sense me through the door every time I came with the groceries, and knew it was me with the food, my nan has a German shepherd, so I am not frightened by them.

'She laughed and just said 'well, Albert you have a friend then.' He sat down and wagged his tail, as if he knew what I had said, of course that is impossible, more than likely he sensed that I did not pose any threat to either him or his owner.

I asked her why she called him Albert? She replied that it was after Albert the Great, she was a history teacher in her working days, she even called her son, who she told me had died in the war, Albert. He loved German Shepard's and they had always had that breed of dog. I thought what a coincidence, after my thoughts about my father and his tales of the war.

After that first encounter, Albert was there at the gate every Saturday waiting for me, to escort me to the door, I even had a coffee with the old woman while my father shagged his lover.

The strange thing was I never asked the old lady her name and she never asked me my name, yet it was like we knew each other.

I was so distrustful of women I never thought I would ever want to choose to be with one. But things went on, and I was popular at the shop that we delivered for, and I dated several girls working there, all of them older than me, one of them I fancied, for once in my life I wanted her to take an interest in me, I dreamt about her touching me and those good feelings being in my control. Unfortunately, she told me she was about to get married, so it remained a purely platonic relationship.

Eventually the shop manager offered me a weekend job in the shop working in the butchery department. He was hoping I might want to work in the shop when I was ready to leave school.

The ceiling in the storeroom remained intact, it did not look as though my father had even remembered he had set it up. I was disappointed, yet again, not getting one over on him.

So, I accepted the offer to work with the shop butcher at the weekend. Back then there were no large shops open on a Sunday, so training was slow. At first, I wasn't sure I could cut up whole animals. I was wrong though, I enjoyed it. I imagined I was cutting him up every time I removed a rib from a pig's carcass.

He still insisted that I went with him on his 'romantic exploits' which gave him cover with my mother, because I was with him, up the pub or at the 'dogs' (greyhound racing), the true explanation being the latter as they were mostly 'dogs.' This always led to the abuse, in whichever way he chose for them to teach me the art of pleasing and being pleased. By now I was just disgusted and enjoyed making them wince as I sucked their nipples hard and pushed as far as I could into their mouths. It's best to use your imagination at this point.

But I must clarify one thing at this point, even though I hated him vigorously for everything he put me through. He never sexually abused me himself, just revelled in what he could get them to do to degrade me.

Then came the fateful night, the night that changed my life. Whether for the better or worse I will never know, because I chose the action which made me into the person I am now and will always be, although I still struggle to control all my actions, and never will be able to.

After the encounter with his latest conquest, I asked to use the bathroom before leaving, I wanted to find some mouthwash to clean out my mouth and decided to look in the bathroom cupboard.

No mouthwash, but I found loads of tablets, some were yellow, some white and some bright red, there was even powder in transparent plastic containers, which was the stuff they used to sniff off the back of their hands. This was the answer, I could take these with me and end my misery, no one would dare to report me if it meant listing the stuff that I had access to.

I would just go to sleep and be at peace, I knew the yellow ones were sleeping tablets, because it was marked on the label, so if I took everything together, no more threats, no more doing what I didn't want to do, no more seeing my mother putting up with the life he was forcing her to live, he will have to face the consequences if I leave a note. No, he would worm his way out of it somehow, anyway I did not have time, I had to act before I lost the courage.

It is not, as people believe, an act of cowardice or selfishness. In my case I did not know how I would ever stop the cycle, but knew I had to stop it in some way, how could I tell my mother everything without destroying her? he was not worth that, it would have just made him more powerful, my logic was simple.

For me to die would have made everyone question why? How would he answer that question or the others who allowed him to ridicule me? It would appear as an act of desperation. Back then there was nowhere to turn, no help in fact no acceptance that this type of emotional and physical depravation was happening. As we find out now, this type of abuse was accepted by the society of the time, the social care was almost zero, run by well-meaning under trained mushrooms (kept in the dark by the governments and fed on bullshit).

Would my death be effective? I did not even consider that question. I just did not know how to end the cycle and trusted no one. I was fast loosing respect for everyone including my mother and sisters. In short, I was becoming just like the arsehole I detested, not what I wanted to be.

I wanted to be someone who would have influence in some way, at some time, even if for just a fleeting moment. By this one act my short life would mean something to someone, if only to make someone aware of what our society was becoming, not this free revolutionary age, just a more sophisticated form of communism and dictatorship. Not that I knew then what those ideals really were, I had just read them somewhere.

Chapter 5

The dark shadow

With my newly acquired solution to end my life, I decided to go to bed early that night under the pretext of having a headache, which I often suffered at that time of my life.

I went up to the bathroom and took all the tablets and powders I had taken from the cabinet, ironically my mother had given me two aspirin to help with my headache, for some reason I did not want to take those, I thought it might come back on my mother in some way. I cut up and flushed all the papers and foil down the toilet.

I then managed to walk from the toilet to my bedroom along the landing, in fact it was a fantastic trip, feeling just like I was walking on air, if this was dying, I wanted to repeat it. I climbed into bed and closed my eyes and for the first time ever, I felt completely at peace, it felt as though I was floating above my body, I could see my body laying below me on the bed completely at peace, eyes closed and a stupid grin on my face, I thought what a fantastic experience.

I did not feel any regret, no pain, just pure joy, as if the whole of the weight of the world had lifted from me. I thought if this were death my only regret was that I could not do it again. Just pure relief that nothing more will ever hurt me, with that nothing, not even blackness, just nothing.

But what seemed instantaneous, my floating body slammed back into the one on the bed laying lifeless. As the two joined together, I felt a presence in the room, I turned only my eyes, as they were the only part of my body I could feel, the rest of my body was not there, I could not feel my body, just the ache in my eyes, a feeling I experienced later.

At the bedroom door, there was a figure, but just a shadow not a solid form, looking over me, he was holding something in his hand. Shit, I thought the bastard has found out what I have done, and he is even going to stop me from having my forever peace.

The shadow began to move around the bed, it had no depth to its form, just a presence there, I could sense there was something in its shadow like hand, I knew it was a knife it was long and straight, just like the ones I used on the carcasses in the shop. I thought, please do not let this be a dream, let him kill me, I cannot wake up, it will all be for nothing. I tried to close my eyes, but they were not part of me, I could not control them even though I could see through them. What was going on?

The figure stopped at the opposite side of the bed to the door, my eyes had followed it around the room, the dark shadow only a picture on the wall, but my head and body did not exist, just my eyes full of tears. Then a black shadow of a head came towards me. I tried to cry out but there was only silence, I tried to move but I had no body to move, I just had blackness and a sense of nothingness.

The shadow then spoke to me in a whisper 'You can`t escape this way.' Shit, I thought what should I do? I know it is too late for him to save me, so why is he here, why can't he just let me go. I can still remember clearly, I thought it was my father, so I was only thinking of why he was beside me, my thoughts were, I know he will try to save me, because he knows they will blame him they will find out what he has been doing, then with hope in my thoughts I prayed that he would just kill me and get away, but I do not want that. I do not want him to control my death. I knew this had to be a dream because I was reasoning with the actions taking place. But it was not like a dream it was real but a reality I could not control.

The voice continued, 'You have a lot to do before we take you, don`t worry it won't be like this forever he will be gone before you know it, in the meantime go by your feelings, never be afraid, listen to your voices within, we will always be there.'

He stood up and I could only see two blood red eyes in the shadow that no longer looked like a human form, just a floating shadow. The same voice continued, 'you will never feel pain like this again, the only real pain you will feel is never being able to be close to the family you have, but you will learn to love, you will know when it comes cherish it.' and with that the shadow raised the long knife and plunged it into my stomach I screamed out in pain, then it lifted the knife again.

Repeatedly, it plunged into my stomach, each time deeper and each time more painful, I screamed so loud I was sure someone would come rushing in and stop it. But it continued until I no longer felt pain just emptiness.

Suddenly only a black cloud hovered above me and was drawn into the gaping hole that appeared in the place my body should have been, and then there was nothing but blackness.

The next thing I knew was, the bed covers moving and a small hand touching my face. I thought I must be in hell because of the darkness I had experienced. But how was I feeling anything if I am dead, I thought, this cannot be.

To my horror I realised it was the hand of my youngest sister. 'What the hell had happened this can`t be possible,' there is no way I could still be here.

She spoke to me, 'are you alright I think you are sad, and I don't want you to be sad, I heard you shout, I think you must have been dreaming.'

I took her hand and kissed it, it felt solid, and I knew that I was alive, I could only manage a feeble 'I am OK.'

She climbed into the bed beside me and lay there in silence. After a while she said, 'don't be sad, I know your sad and you are white, probably because you are cold, you smell funny as well, have you been sick? Shall I tell mummy you are sick.' 'No, no I said it's just a tummy bug I will be ok.' How ironic a big tummy bug I thought.

She got up from the bed and went back to her room. I felt a strange sensation at that moment, a feeling that I knew her, of course I did she was my sister. But it was a feeling that she was from my past, or my future, it was as if, she knew something was wrong and wanted to protect me. I did not want to feel close to her, I was sure I was dead, I must be. I had done enough to kill myself and be free from this life that I hated so much.

I fell back into the blackness and the next thing I knew was my mother shaking me. Jill tells me you are sick, so you had better stay in bed, I do not want the girls getting ill she said, then went out and closed the door.

It was then I was finally convinced that I was not dead, but how come? I had felt as though my stomach was about to blow open, but my head was clear, nothing had changed. Where do I go from here, I thought?

Of course, back then there was not the information available on media to find out exactly what I had taken, I found out much later that the mixture of drugs and birth control pills I had taken should have killed me instantaneously. Instead, it unlocked something that will stay with me forever and has shaped my life, although up to now I still do not truly know how to control it or understand the true potential of this legacy. It seems to change as the years pass, intense in the beginning without being able to control it at all, but feeling the power of having it with me, no fear of pain but no understanding of why not.

Then to a stage where I almost came to understand how to control it. But could never actually get true control. If I managed to get the effect I wanted, the same action next time did nothing. Total control was always just out of my reach.

Later still I lost the intensity and urgency to understand and control it. But still now and probably until the end of my life I will always strive to get the power it gave me back and under control.

So, I will continue with my story, you may have had a similar experience, because as I get older, I read and hear accounts from surprising sources that almost match my own experiences.

Taking you back, when I eventually emerged from

my bedroom, my mother commented that I looked green and half asleep, and she said that would keep me off school for the week, as I must have picked up a bug, I laughed inside, some bug, something burrowed in my stomach, it was not a bug that is for sure, but whatever it was it had failed to do what I had planned, to give me eternal peace.

The rest of the day I felt good, in fact I did not even have a headache, which I thought was strange before I was always getting headaches. When I went to bed, I was calm and did not think about the night before, but I could not get the shadow out of my head. What was it? It was so real I even heard it speak. What did it mean? Never be afraid, listen to your voices within, we will always be there.' Who are we? Is their more than one of these things floating around?

There was no way back then you could get help. I would have been sent to a psychiatric hospital and disappeared into the masses that were put quietly away from society. God only knows what happened to those children who found abuse at the hands of the so-called pillars of society, even the church, claimed to only discovered later on in the years to come and even then, not the full extent of the suffering endured.

These were violent days, a lot of things were beginning to happen in the world, things that were now being transmitted on the news stations. Many things would later trigger off memories of exactly what you were doing when they happened. I was in the back room watching television with my pal Joe at his house, when it was televised that President John F. Kennedy had been assassinated, this was on November 22, 1963, at 12:30 p.m. I was 12 years old.

He was riding in a motorcade in Dallas during a campaign visit. Kennedy's motorcade was at Dealey Plaza where crowds were lining the streets, shots were heard. Realising the shots had been at the car the driver of the president's limousine, with its top open, raced to nearby Parkland Memorial Hospital.

Kennedy was shot in the neck and head. He was pronounced dead at 1 p.m. He was 46 years old. The president's assassination was to have a profound political and cultural impact on the U.S.A nation.

Within about an hour and a half of the shooting, Lee Harvey Oswald, a new employee at the Book Depository, near Dealey Plaza was arrested for JFK's assassination, along with the fatal shooting of a Dallas patrolman.

Two days later, in November 24, Oswald was shot at point blank range by local nightclub owner and police informant Jack Ruby.

Oswald was born in New Orleans in 1939. His father died of a heart attack two months before he was born. He moved with his mother to New York at age 12, where he was sent to a youth detention centre for truancy. It was during this time that he became interested in Socialism. After moving back to New Orleans, Oswald joined the Marines in 1956, where he qualified as a sharpshooter, and discovered Marxism.

In 1959 he received an early honourable discharge from the Marines, he then defected to Russia, where he was denied citizenship, but was allowed to stay in the country, reputedly under close monitoring by the K.G.B. Russia's state police.

When it was discovered that Oswald had wanted to defect, the Marines downgraded his discharge from 'honourable' to 'undesirable' in 1962. Later that year, Oswald returned to Texas with his Soviet wife and young daughter.

Oswald tried to shoot, Major General Edwin A. Walker who had been a staunch critic of Communism and later in 1963, Oswald was denied passage to Cuba and the U.S.S.R. He returned to Texas and started a job at the Texas School Book Depository in Dallas.

According to the official investigation, Oswald acted alone, firing three bullets from a sixth-floor window at the southeast corner of the Book Depository. Kennedy was struck once in the upper back and once in the head and slumped over onto his wife, Jacqueline Kennedy.

Texas Governor John B. Connally Jr., who was also in the limo with his wife, was shot once in the back. He recovered from his injuries.

The Vice President Lyndon B. Johnson and his wife had been three cars behind Kennedy in the motorcade. They returned to Air Force One at

Dallas Love Field, with Kennedy's body, in a bronze casket.

Johnson was sworn in at 2:38 p.m. as the 36th president of the United States while aboard the airplane prior to take-off. Jacqueline Kennedy, still in a pink suit splattered with blood, stood at Johnson's side. An autopsy on Kennedy's body was performed at Bethesda Naval Hospital in Maryland. During his interrogation, Oswald denied any guilt, saying 'I didn't shoot anybody'.

Back to life in the U.K where luckily it wasn't as easy to shoot someone as it appeared to be in some other countries, back then I didn't even dream I would ever visit the U.S.A. I am happy that I eventually visited almost every state through my work, meeting people from all walks of life there.

Chapter 6

Was this the beginning?

Monday morning, I was back at school and deciding if I should tell my best friend Joe about what I had done and my experience with the dark shadow, but then quickly remembered that he knew nothing of the depth of my problems at home. Later, I told him some of the lesser things I had experienced.

He knew of the horrible things my father was capable of, we even went on later, to have great laughs at his expense, in fact on many occasions. One of the funnier ones being the time he decided he would repair a puncture in his car tyre. He had removed the wheel from the car and used tyre leavers to get the tire out of the rim. He had bought a new innertube (still used in those bygone days). But when he tried to replace the tyre after inserting the innertube, he found it much more difficult to replace the tyre over the new innertube than remove it.

He tried using the leavers he had bought specially to remove the tyre, bearing in mind these were for use without an innertube, so he decided to get extra leverage, to allow for the innertube now fitted to the rim, he would use a garden shovel. With the greater purchase on the tyre, and after a struggle, the tyre fitted into the rim.

He was ecstatic at his achievement. Joe and I had watched the whole episode and were impressed with his perseverance. He fitted the foot pump and began pumping up the tyre then it happened. You could hear the hiss of air escaping from the tyre, he had punctured the new innertube with the sharp edge of the shovel.

He went berserk and while his huge eighteen stone frame leaped on the wheel, simultaneously he wielded the shovel overhead and brought it down on the tyre, in the process he scored the ceiling. After the third strike we decided to make an exit, we could no longer contain ourselves.

We went out the back door and managed to get out into the alley way between our house and the next-door neighbours, just before we degenerated into uncontrollable laughter, I am sure if he would had seen us, I would have received a beating.

Talking about beating, the first of my bad encounters with the darkness happened at once after this incident.

All our class at school, had invitations to an

organised youth dance at the local church hall, my best friend Joe could not go but I went with a couple of other school friends. I was not particularly interested in girls and certainly had zero interest in young giggly ones. Some of the boys had girlfriends, and one of the classmates came along with his girlfriend, as part of our group.

As the night went on boys arrived from local youth clubs some older than us and one had an eye on the girl with us.

She decided during the evening to go to the toilet and when she came out, the guy I noticed eying her up, decided he would harass her, my friend asked him very nicely to leave her alone. Instead, he grabbed her and kissed her, my friend stood back and looked down. Suddenly I felt a strange sensation, like a darkness descending, the next thing I knew the guy was lying on the floor, his friends picked him up and said to me 'outside you bastard we are going to kill you.'

I counted six of them, so I said to my school friends, 'who's coming out with me'? There was a dead silence, 'run out the back way' one of them said. I normally would have done just that but this time a voice in my head told me. You wanted to die? let us see how easy it is. So, I went outside.

The biggest one in the gang was leaning against the wall, he moved slightly away from it leaving around a 6-inch gap, I did not even think I just ran at him and drove his head back against the wall, my fist, driving into his face.

He was obviously the leader of the pack as the rest stood paralysed for a few seconds, just enough time for me to drive my foot into the knee of the second boy, which resulted in him collapsing on the floor writhing in agony.

That is when my luck ran out and I learnt for sure that six against one did not compute to a sensible expectation of winning the contest. I felt the blows, but it never really hurt, I managed to cover my head and face and then I heard them shout 'quick fucking cop`s'.

I managed to get to my feet and stagger up the road, noting the two big guys were still out on the grass, one clutching his knee and screaming.

The next day when I woke up in bed, I just couldn`t move. My mother called the doctor to check me over, I had told her I that I had fallen down some stairs and admitted to drinking some cider.

The doctor checked me over and with a smile said, 'how many? You should report this to the police, you don`t get bruises like that from falling downstairs, I assured him that at least two of them were worse off than me, he just tutted and said with a sigh, 'I had better give you a poultice for the bruised ribs and tell your mum to keep you off school for the rest of the week'. You don`t find doctors like that anymore, he was a hero.

I decided that I would try to tell my best mate some of my experience of the past few days and something was different about me, but how do you start without divulging things in your life that should always remain, only in your own head and heart. luckily not long after this incident odd things happened in his presence that made him question me about what was happening to me, not that I knew myself.

He knew me well and realised I was not the norm if there is such a person as normal. If we were making weapons for a game, he would make a gun shape out of wood and fix a wooden bayonet to it, I would make a wooden gun and invent a firing system using elastic bands, to fire wooden bullets. Mine took ages to make, while he had made his and killed me three times before I could pull back the band and load the wooden bullet.

I learned from it but even so, only that my bayonet had to be detachable, so I could use the firing system if I wanted to. I also liked to make the Dutch arrow, which was a straight piece of branch the diameter of an arrow, about a quarter of the full length from the tip of the arrow I made a small notch, this notch housed a string with a knot in the end of it. The knot sat at the notch and the string had one turn around the arrow diameter and across the knot, which you then held the string tightly against the arrow shaft putting tension on the knot sitting at the notch. Now you stepped forward and launched the arrow at the target. When you had mastered the throw, the acceleration on the arrow was phenomenal and became a dangerous weapon in the wrong hands, such as me. Fortunately, I never had the need to use one in anger.

Getting back to Joe. He would punch me or wrestle with me, while I would bend his thumbs back, which was far more vicious. Having said all this, we were closer than real brothers and always had a good laugh together.

There are a few of the funny incidents just to break up the intensity of my earlier pages. We decided that it might be fun to get inside a water butt and roll it over the small wall that separated the top lawn from the lower level. We decided it would be better to convince the boy living next door to Joe, to try out this fantastic ride, after exaggerating this adventure ride of a lifetime, he climbed in, full of excitement. We began the roll of the butt, and he went down the lawn accelerating towards the wall, where he took off into the air and travelled about five feet before hitting the ground and shattering the barrel into pieces. The poor lad was terrified, even though we congratulated him with the same enthusiasm as you would an astronaut returning to the earth from space.

We of course never were able to get him to join in with our fun games after that, so we had to find our own enjoyment together.

Even now I find our escapades much funnier than Joe ever did, mainly because he got the worse end of the deal, I guess.

On one such occasion, we decided we would play tag on roller skates around his house, I was often there as I preferred it to being at my house. Unfortunately, we only had one pair of skates between us, so we had one each.

We were racing around his house and driveway on the one skate when a couple of girls came into the garden delivering leaflets, these were girls of the same year as us, and as I came around the corner, I caught sight of them, just in time to stop and hide up the skate and act cool.

'Hi there, I said, we don't usually have such attractive girls come to see us', they both smiled sweetly, but just after I had finished my sick chat up line, Joe came around the corner in full flight shouting, 'got you, got you, your it, your it', he stopped in full stride and crashed into me, we fell to the ground in a tangle exposing both skates. The girls burst into laughter, leaving us both feeling like a couple of idiots. From then on, we got a snigger, from them and their friends every time we saw them at school.

Luckily, they did not see him swinging between the gate posts the next day, resulting in him swinging too high and collapsing in a heap onto the concrete pavement banging the back of his head. I managed to stifle a giggle for around 30 seconds, but I could not contain myself when he stood up in a wobbly way and said fuck me !! before bursting into fits of uncontrollable laughter with me.

He got his own back doubly though, the first was an encounter with a gang of lads from our class, in a place we called the public open space, which was a wood and field area where all the local youth, many from our school, went to meet up play games and be stupid.

We had heard from an unknown source, that the woods were haunted at dusk by ghosts that came out to terrorise anyone in there, I have not a clue who started the rumour in the first place, or why. We did not believe it, of course, but a lot appeared to, or they were part of the prank. So, Joe and I decided that we would play along with the lads and when we got a chance, would play a prank on them by pretending to be a couple of the ghosts.

We hung back whilst our friends went off armed with clubs in the form of bits of wood to deal with the ghosts, strange as ghosts are supposed to have no solid form.

Dismissing this knowledge, we took a short cut to a path that we knew the lads would come down in their search for the ghouls. As they came past the area, we were hiding in the bushes.

I leapt out screaming, never contemplating the reaction of one of the guys. He turned and at the same time lashed out with the piece of wood, which struck me straight on the right-hand side of the head, within seconds a lump the size of a bolder appeared. Everyone was aghast for about the time it took the lump to form then as quickly turned to uncontrollable laughter instigated by Joe himself, retribution for my reaction at the gate no doubt. Painful but it quickly deflated leaving a large bruise.

In the same area only days later we had threats, by a gang of boys one of them carrying a pellet gun. He threatened to shoot us unless we gave him something, full of my newfound courage and stupidity, I decided I would take the gun from him, so as he pushed the barrel of the pistol against my ribcage, I grabbed it and twisted it away from me.

Unfortunately, I learnt that you cannot take a gun from a person when it is pressed against you, unless it is in a film script, in fact the action causes it to go off, luckily, I managed to get the pellet out as it was only a 0.177 calibre, but it was sore for days after, but who cared, it was the joy of growing up. We had many laughs, some at the expense of my mate Joe, and some at me. Some incidents will always remain in our memories, like the one below.

We were on holiday at Portland bill, a destination that was one of our favourites. My father never took us away for holidays, just days out ending up in a pub with a slot machine. Joes' parents however included me in their holiday plans and treated me kindly. This time we were camping, and it was raining heavily, even so we decided to walk into Weymouth town to get a couple of models to construct.

We liked to make the plastic airplanes and paint them, but this time we found some horror figures to assemble. As usual we both liked the same figure, the hunchback of Notre dame, so we tossed a coin to see who got the figure as it was the last one in the shop. Joe won the toss of the coin and got the coveted hunchback; I took the mummy. All the way back Joe was goading me, mainly because I usually won the toss up, so he was feeling happy that he had got his desired figure and I had to settle for second best.

We got back to the caravan, and both eagerly opened the boxes, very quickly Joe discovered that one of the main parts of his model was missing, 'the hump.'

He went berserk, I couldn't keep a straight face after a quip about not getting the 'ump and after a desperate attempt to look sad for him I burst into uncontrollable laughter. The more I tried to stifle my mirth the more I laughed.

Eventually he stormed off and sheepishly returned soaked through. This was in 1966, the year that England won the football world cup, we watched on the television in a pub on Portland bill. I later joked with my son's, that they would probably never see the football World cup, be won by England. I hope I am wrong!!

Later, in this story, even this year, date, and location feature in a large part of my life, just a coincidence? or destiny, when you get to the part in the story, you can decide for yourself. Unfortunately, because of the length of time in different situations I do jump backwards and forwards a little in time, but you can stick with it, everything catches up by the end of the story.

We were undergoing a significant leap in technological advancements worldwide during the late 50`s and 60`s.

In 1957 the first live animal was sent into space, it was a dog called Laika, sent into orbit on the 3rd of November, on bord Sputnik 2, a Russian space achievement. Unfortunately, Laika died in orbit, but the space race was on. August 1960 saw dogs Belka and Stpelka along with a rabbit, 42 mice, two rats and a bunch of fruit flies sent into orbit. This time the craft Sputnik 5 returned to Earth with all the passengers alive. Russia was leading the space race.

But not for long U.S.A, could not allow that, so in January 1961 Mercury-Redstone was sent into orbit with a U.S Airforce Chimpanzee on board. One up on Russia and the closest to mankind, paving the way, to put a human being on the Moon.

So, back to this holiday in the west, it was full of surprises and near disasters and not just the one featuring the model of the hunchback. We decided to go fishing, another of our favourite pastimes, both sea and freshwater, of course this incident happened whilst fishing in the sea.

We had found a large rock just around fifty feet from the cliffs. We strapped the collapsed rods and a knapsack over our shoulders. Off we swam to the rock, which took a noticeably fleeting period of time. We then spent a lengthy period fishing and sunbathing. Eventually the sea was almost up to the top of the rock, so we decided to pack up the Knapsacks and swim back, as we both entered the water a large wave swept us out from the rock, both of us were good swimmers for our age, but no matter how hard we swam we just remained the same distance from the shoreline. Both of us were getting tired and beginning to feel a little panic setting in, it was strange to have a feeling that whatever you did your energy was sapping but the distance to travel was the same.

I told Joe to hold on to me and we would kick together, I do not know why I suggested this, other than just a wild desperate idea I had.

But sure enough, either by luck, or the tide had slightly changed, we began to get to the edge of chesil beach. It was crazy, the rock itself looked just a few feet from the mainland, but it looked miles from the point we had eventually landed on the beach. We were both wasted from fear than actual physical tiredness. And we still had to walk back to the campsite. The whole incident taught us to respect the power of the sea.

Whenever I hear the news about a drowning, or see a programme on rescues at sea, I can understand how simple it is for something that seems safe and fun, to change into a complete disaster, putting your own and sometimes, others' lives in danger. How did we survive? Luck or fate, who knows, but not long after this episode, things became even more strange.

Joe had a female cousin, who with her mother lived with Joes parents, she was around six years older than us and was like a big sister.

Chapter 7

To the table

Dina did all the things big sisters do, like spoil our games, tease us about girls etc, but being older she was out meeting older boys, one of these was to eventually become her husband, his name was also Keith, he had a sister and a brother, his brother was at our school and around our age, he also became a part of our small band.

It is odd but all through our school days we had other boys, in our school year and even after leaving school, that we hung around with, but they all came and went while we remained together.

Getting back to Keith's brother, I must admit he was a little odd and gullible, but that is another story. This is part of the progression into a strange world for me, began when we started spending time at their house.

His mother and sister were, like a lot of people at that time, interested in the supernatural, So, his mother decided she would like to organise a séance, this included ourselves, Clive, and joe's cousin. The table was set out with cards that had numbers and letters on them, there was a wine glass placed upside down in the centre of the table.

The idea was that everyone around the table would put a finger onto the glass, just touching the edge of the base.

Someone was nominated, to ask a question, one that only that person would know the answer to.

The answer to the question would be given by the spirit, through the person chosen by it to be the messenger. This was the odd thing; a person was not chosen beforehand to be the messenger, but would naturally become one, by elimination.

The next stage was that the question would be by someone nominated, that person would write down the answer, so nobody could see it. It would be revealed, once the answer was given by the stopping of the glass at various letters and numbers.

Each letter or number, written down and the answer presented to the questioner, to verify it`s accuracy.

I had decided that this was a situation that could be the perfect opportunity for a prank, I would make up the first thing, which came into my head as the answer to any question asked. Well of course it started out difficult, because this was obviously not meant to be a source of fun, but one of a serious scientific nature, led by and controlled by Keith's Mum. So, the first question was from her.

I thought to myself this will be interesting, as I know absolutely zero about the family and certainly nothing whatsoever about Keith`s mother, nevertheless I thought it would still be fun and hopefully she would forgive me once we had a good laugh.

The question was, 'what was my father`s pet name for me? I decided to move the glass to the letters making up just the first name that came into my head. Nobody else seemed to have volunteered to answer, so there was no resistance on the glass movement.

With that her face changed, she looked quite concerned at first, then she said 'ok that's correct so I think it's got to be one of you' pointing around to her daughter, Clive, and Keith, you must have heard grandad joking with me and one of you has remembered. All three of them denied knowing the answer and I knew they were telling the truth.

She was a little put out and I did not really want to play, because it looked like she was taking it all too seriously, and when she finds out I was only joking, she will be even more annoyed. Should I own up now and save my embarrassment?

She then continued, so I am going to tell you three to remove your fingers from the glass, and I will ask another question.

I must admit I felt a little bit uncomfortable because she seemed quite upset and a little annoyed that she thought her children were making fun of her.

They tried to assure her they did not know her pet name and had never heard it from their grandfather. But it was clear that this was the only explanation in her mind. She had obviously been certain, when she decided to use that name as a sign that a spirit was in the room, that nobody would have known the answer.

I later discovered that she had done this before with her friend, who was a practicing medium, and this immediate success was not what she was expecting. She insisted they remove their fingers from the glass which left her, me, Joe, and Joe's cousin who also knew extraordinarily little about the family.

What she did not realise was that the most surprised person around the table was me. Now she will know which one of us was the one playing around. At least she won't be sure of which one, I thought. I had not even considered the question that would have been in her mind if it was not them. Who knew the answer?

We decided to continue, mainly because no one wanted to upset her, least of all me because it looked like my innocent prank was going to backfire big time. We placed our fingers on the top of the glass and the next question that she asked was quite surprising and would end the game, she was obviously more annoyed at being the butt of a joke than I had expected her to be, this was serious stuff.

Her question was 'what is my bank balance' as of today. Well, this was great there is no way that I could get this right, so I pushed the glass to random numbers.

This was not a simple selection of numbers because, I did not want to insult her, by pointing to numbers giving a low figure, but I also did not want to go way over the top with a number that obviously was ridiculously high, so I just picked a figure out of the air, it was in the low hundreds say £400, I also added a few Pence just to make it look good, this was my mistake.

She wrote the figure down, then she got up from the table and went to the sideboard, she opened a draw and removed a piece of paper, opened the paper, and said nothing. She returned to her seat and told Joe and his cousin not to touch the glass. This left just me and her. She asked another question about the pattern and colour on a jumper of hers. Should I really continue, or just admit to the pranks, but then by her actions she knows it is me, so what, the money must have been wrong and now she is going to turn the tables on me, she does not even own a white cashmere jumper.

Again, I thought of the first thing that came into my head. This time as I pushed the glass, I could feel she was pushing against the glass in the opposite direction, so I put more pressure on and tried to divert it to the position I was heading for in the first place, as I did her finger came off the glass and it flew across the table and smashed against the sideboard.

There was complete silence in the room, she looked at me and opened, the piece of paper from the sideboard draw, it was her latest statement and on the statement was the same figure I had written on the paper, everyone was surprised, me included. She looked at me in a strange way saying. 'I did not even know the figure on my statement, it only came just before you all arrived, that is why I had to look first. I need to talk with my friend, then can we have another séance?' We all agreed, although I doubted that I could guess again so accurately but thought Joe and I could dream up an extension to the prank I had just played.

Little did I know that this would be the beginning of a strange sequence of events that would lead me to believe that something deeply disturbing, happened to me during my encounter with the drugs and the appearance of the apparition in my room.

It was just a week later that Joe Clive and me, were going fishing at the weekend, we enjoyed fishing in one of the small lakes close to where we lived. We usually had quite a laugh at Clive's expense, like all boys of our age we were very quick to make people the butt of our jokes, simply because they were different to us in the way they executed things.

Clive's mother was very strange in lots of ways, one being the way she would prepare his sandwiches in a little box, with them and the rest of the contents, would be a menu of the precise contents of the box.

Joe and I of course made our own lunches and consisted of massive great big wedges of bread and cheese and an apple wrapped up in a brown paper bag. We found it very strange that the sandwiches were so neatly made each one cut as a triangle. Clive would sit down with his little napkin on his knee and read his menu, then eat it in the same sequence as the menu.

After eating our lunches, we began fishing again, unfortunately Clive's fishing line caught in the reeds, so he decided he would try to release it. He found a short plank which was on the bank of the lake and laid it across to the position where his line was caught, then asked Joe if he would stand on the end of the plank while he walked out to try to release the line. He then looked at Joe as if something had crossed his mind and said, 'you promise you won't jump off.' Joe looked at me as if a light had just switched on in his head, smiled and said of 'course I won't.' As you have already guessed, as soon as he reached the end of the plank, Joe pretended that he slipped off the plank, and Clive was up to his waste in the freezing chilly water.

There was no way that we could hide our amusement at the situation, and I do not think Clive trusted us ever again, although we still hung around together. He was a good-looking guy and could always get the girls flocking around.

Most of the times after a period of conversation with the three of us, the girls decided that he was all looks and not much else, so most times we ended up with the pick of the available 'fruit,' so to speak.

Yes, you are right I was a chauvinist back then. Joe and I were invited back to Clive's house for the return séance, there was a lot of eager anticipation at what would happen this time, but there were new rules, no cards, no numbers, and no glasses. Clive's mother decided that I should be, assessed because she believed, after talking to her friend that I had some sort of spiritual power.

Chapter 8

Return to the table

This time we all sat around the table with our hands touching in a circle and we began. Clive's mother asked if the spirit was here and if it was, she had a task for it to perform through its medium. I looked over at Joe and like me he was not expecting this to happen, we had hatched a plan and had a few signs, like two blinks for yes and three for no. Well now was the time for me to get my comeuppance, how embarrassing this was going to be.

I was about to own up for my childish prank at our first séance, when Clive's mother suddenly said, 'but first we have to say the Lord's prayer.' Her friend the medium had told her that this protects against evil spirits, so as we were going into an unknown situation, she wanted us to be safe. I of course was amused at this but tried to suppress my mirth. So, we all recited the Lord's prayer. I must say I do not really know or understand what happened from then on, or exactly what was said, I do know what I felt, but I really did not understand what was going on and even to this day I still wonder whether it happened or whether it was just a figment of my imagination. However, Joe and his cousin assure me it happened. You will have to judge for yourself.

Clive's mother sat opposite me and simply asked in her normal way 'who are you and why are you here?' There was no strange feeling, it was just like having a simple conversation, but I was full of confidence and all the other people in the room were there, but seemed frozen, no movements but I knew they were there.

I replied, with something like a script out of a play. 'You called me to you.'

'But who are you.' asked Clive's mum, 'I am the protector of the spirit in this body, I come from a long time ago.' I was off to a good start, all totally improvised, as I could not even communicate with Joe, everyone was just a blur. So, do I leave it there or push it a bit? No, I think I will play it safe and just ask a question 'What do you want me to do, to prove that I'm here, something you can take back to silly old Mrs Marchant.' Clive's mother looked visibly shocked, but surprisingly re-claimed her composure. I on the other hand was feeling odd, I could not blink, and my eyes were watering, the tears running down my face.

At this point, despite feeling odd I assumed that Clive's mother believed Joe and myself were in this together, so she asked Joe to give her a number, any number that came into his head, I do not remember what that number was, but she then handed me a sheet of paper and a pen and asked me to write down the psalm from the Bible, that equated to the number Joe had just given her, I think it was 101 but I have never been sure. Joe remembers to this day.

Well, I thought this is the end of our little game, but I had better give her something, otherwise it will be embarrassing for her, and make me look like an idiot. So, I began writing down words that came into my head on to the paper. All the time I was writing the words down on the paper, tears were rolling down my cheeks and I could not blink my eyes, in fact they were becoming sore.

I put down the pen and everyone around the table was staring at me. 'You can go now' said Clive's mother, In a matter-of-fact way. I felt an immediate sense of anger and found I was replying. 'I will decide when I go not you, my power is far greater than yours, you called me, I decide when I go.' They all began to recite something on a piece of paper in front of them, I found out later that it was the Lord's prayer written backwards. My anger increased and I suddenly felt vulnerable and threatened, I did not know where I was, my prank had turned into panic and then there was darkness. It seemed like a space of just nothingness.

Suddenly I could blink my eyes, Clive's mother put her arm around me and asked me if I was OK, she kept saying she was sorry for not believing me. I did not have a clue about what she was talking about.

Just breathe deeply she said and then she told Joe to open the bible in front of him and read out the psalm he had given her the number of, as he got to about the tenth word, she decided to continue reading my words aloud herself. I did not understand what she ment, until everyone was shown the piece of paper on which I had written. Although the writing was very untidy, I had written down word for word the psalm Joe had given the number of. I do not know how it happened, but I never read the bible let alone memorised every psalm in it.

It did not end here of course, unfortunately most of the people around the table believed that Joe and I had somehow pulled off this prank especially Clive, who had been on the end of many of our premeditated pranks. So, Clive's mother decided that the only way to prove it was all genuine we had to meet the famous Ms Marchant and put an end to it.

We had not considered the consequences of what we would find out. But now I needed to know, was it linked to the man with the knife in my dream? Had I become slightly unstable or was it something special that would remain with me, good or bad, for the rest of my life.

The only things I knew for sure, were that I did not memorise any Psalm, there were no hand signs or winks between me and Joe, I could not blink my eyes, but I knew everything I said, and it was me saying it. I never at any stage thought there was another presence, it was me but somehow detached from my body.

I will tell you right now, after the final one, which I describe below, never have I ever had a séance again.

I will never forget what happened over those few days and what has happened since which continues as part of this Storey.

Chapter 9

The trumpet

We arrived at Ms Marchant's house, she was around the same age as Clive's mother and was very relaxed. She offered us a Cup of tea before we began, although she seemed very calm, I could sense she was excited that I was there.

On the table there was a bunch of Flowers and a cardboard cone turned upside down. It had a red stripe painted around it's circumference, in a spiral from the pointed end to the base. After drinking our tea's and eating the delicious cream cakes that she had provided, she turned directly to me and said, 'you'll be safe here, are you happy to go ahead with this because it can be very frightening and I know the last time you had lost control, but that's because you are very young.' She sounded extremely excited, like a child who had just received a present, she had always dreamed of. 'What did it feel like? I believe what I am told about you, but you do know I will be able to tell if the spirit is coming through you, or you are just playing games.' It seemed like she was doubting that I was genuine, but at the same time was hopeful that this could be a new experience for her.

I on the other hand was sure I was now about to be exposed, as a prankster. But I had gone too far to back out now. Why was I doing this, was it because for once in my life I felt special, I was clever enough now to fool everyone, just like my father was. But one better, hold an audience and have everyone in it believing I was special. A greater achievement than he could ever reach. I had to continue, now was my time.

We sat at our places around the table, I was sitting opposite Ms Marchant, to her left was Joe and to her right Clive's mother. We all spread out our palms with our thumb touching thumb and small fingers touching small fingers of the person next to us, in the centre of the circle we had formed, was the cone I had spotted. What was this for.

As at our previous séance, Mrs Marchant, Joe and Clive's mother, recited the Lord's prayer, as they were doing this the strange thing was, I did not feel frightened or worried about what I was going to say, it was quite comforting that I had a voice in my head saying this is going to be okay I think you can fool this woman quite easily let us see what we can do.

Her first question was 'How do we call you to our world?' I answered at once, 'you call us through the trumpet, although we are here all the time.' There was absolute silence, Ms Marchant looked visibly shocked, but only briefly, she composed herself and continued. I felt far away and experienced a strange feeling of power within me, one of complete control. She looked as if she was trying to come to terms with a situation that she had met before, but far less intent. She then went on, 'where is the trumpet?' I answered as if we were just having a normal conversation. 'That pathetic cardboard cone with the red stripe.' She seemed to begin enjoying herself and asked me, 'What is your name and where are you from?' 'Donavan, I replied, I am from your distant past and am preparing to return soon, as one of the chosen few. Do you know what that means or is that beyond your comprehension?'

She was very calm, unlike me who could now feel tears running down my cheeks because I could not blink my eyes. 'Tell me more' she said, almost excited. I began speaking, I remember what I said to this day, but it was a long time before I understood the meaning of what I had said.

'If you don`t know, then you are the one lacking knowledge of your time, how do just a few people borne and living in your time zones, know things far beyond the knowledge of the masses? Let me tell you, just a few of us will never really, what you call die. We just rest until we are called back. A different time a different form, a different purpose. This passage I am in will be one of the chosen pathways in the future, nothing is what it appears to be. Look to a cloudless sky in the darkness of night, what do you see? Thousands upon thousands of lights, but these lights are other worlds and most of them are no longer there. Some have been replaced with new worlds, but you may never see them because their light will take a lifetimes to show it before this planet dies. Now I am going before you need to pretend to send me away, my passage will always be clear.'

With that I was able to blink my eyes. I knew everything I had said but understood nothing. I would, from then on, always strive to understand, the words I spoke at the table amid the flow of tears.

I could hear voices in the distance, it was the three of them reciting the Lord's prayer backwords, I only know that because they told me that had protected me. But I never felt under threat. Their words got louder and louder until I heard Ms Marchant say 'Keith, Keith are you here, are you back with us.' I replied yes, but apart from my sore eyes, I was convinced that I was the one answering the questions and making all the statements and had never gone anywhere, what was I doing? Was I going mad, why had I taken all those tablets? They must be starting to take me over, was it worth it.

We then had the inquest, Ms Marchant was convinced that a spirit had been talking through me, she claimed that only another clairvoyant or a spirit could have known about the trumpet.

It was then that I thought I had better come clean and confess that everything I said was false. After I had explained that it was meant to be just a prank and it had got out of hand. She smiled and then claimed that was impossible and that I had some sort of natural power.

As we left her house, she said to me. 'What was his name?' I automatically answered without any thought. 'Donavan.'

We all went back to our homes and the next day I went down to Joe's house, as I did most weekends and evenings. We sat up in his bedroom, I was sitting at the bottom of his bed and above him at the top of the bed, was a shelf full of books. We sat there having discussions about what had happened the day before, trying to understand why my eyes were watering, even if it could have been that she had been preparing onions for her dinner and I was sensitive to them. Why I was conscious all the time. How I knew everything I said, and apart from not being able to blink, it was just like everything I was saying, I had made up.

Nobody was beside me, I did not sense anything strange, not even the presence of someone else in the room and I certainly did not know why I said the name Donavan, when she asked me his name, strangely enough later in the year I discovered there was a pop singer who called himself Donavan, perhaps I had seen his name in the paper or on the television. Much later still, when I decided to research everything in my young life I discovered, much more relevant to the séance, there was a medieval king back in the 10th century, his name. You are right Donavan.

We had almost convinced ourselves that we had got them all fooled and could have a lot more fun out of the situation. I joked with Joe and said, 'If all this was true then I could move one of your books off the shelf from here.'

He laughed and I stared at one of the books, suddenly a light green haze surrounds the book and the next instant it dropped from the shelf into Joe's lap. Joe jumped up saying 'fuck me' I echoed the sentiment and we both ran from the room.

From that day on, I was obsessed with replicating what had happened, every day and later, every week, I could concentrate on objects and a green haze would appear around them, even today I can get as far as the green haze, but never to the next step. I could never move them.

I say that because what follows in the next chapters are odd incidents that isolated, as they were, could have been caused by chance and my black times just a loss of self-control. But I always remember specific words I said during the encounter with Donovan. 'I am from your distant past and am preparing to return soon, as one of the chosen few. Do you know what that means or is that beyond your comprehension?' And 'Just a few of us will never really die in your understanding, we just rest until we come back through the passage. This passage I am in, will be one of the chosen pathways in the future.' And even more poignant, how do just a few people borne and living in your time zones, know things far beyond the knowledge of the masses? Remember, just a few of us will never die. These words feature a lot in dreams during my life.

Further on in this story, I joke with my sister-in-law about my ascension through the zones, she of course does not know any of this story yet, hopefully if she gets to read it, she will be understanding the significance of Donovan's words.

Getting back to the story, those few days of excitement were lost in the normal day to day lives of us all, Clive`s mother kept wanting us to have more séances, but I was always able to have an excuse not to. Clive went to college to study hairdressing and the worst thing, Joe left school to work for his father.

My father was still the same and refused to let me leave school and work for Joe`s dad, even though he was going to pay for us to attend college to get a brick layers apprenticeship. I must admit my preference was to leave, but then my life would have been different again, this was one of the clear path choices that decide your destiny.

School was never that bad for me, so I will give some high points, some Joe experienced with me, and some happened after he had left. I have put them all together to give an idea of school in our era, we had corporal punishment, as well as dodgy teachers, horses for courses back then. Was it better or worse? I do not know but I would say simply different, we all competed for the same things as now, just that in our day practical positions were more readily available.

So back to the story and schooldays in the start of a most exciting and liberating period of time, still with the same incompetent political parties with their fair share of incompetent politicians, but more significant political parties to choose from. Later there was to become only the realistic choice of two

Chapter 10

Macbreath

I enjoyed drawing, craft work, woodwork, and metal work. And was told by our art teacher that I had every chance of being accepted into art college, he even asked if he could keep one of my pieces of artwork at the end of the year.

Because my father earned a good wage, he had the last say, as he had to contribute to the fees. So, I had to stay on at school for another year and take the GCSE`s, and to study for the preparation of taking an examination, to get an apprenticeship at the local dockyard in Chatham.

There are a couple of incidents, I think are worth including in this story, they are to do with what was called 'the arts sections of our education.' These included fine art, pottery, woodwork, metalwork, and drama.

Both these following incidents involved the teacher of pottery and clay modelling, who also doubled up as the drama teacher. He was a small man although full of himself and unfortunately for him had exceptionally bad breath.

So much so he had the nickname of, breath of death, shortened to Bod. This ensured that there was no chance of him knowing boys pinching their noses and repeating bod, bod, body in a melodic way, had anything to do with him, we even had a complete set of tunes that fitted his actions at the time. This ment that there was not the remotest chance of him realising it was purely an insult to him.

As I say he was an obnoxious little man who enjoyed shaming anyone of us boys who was taller than him, unfortunately for us that was 90% of us. One of his favourite put downs, was to push our heads into the clay bin, following throwing down a pot that had to be dumped into the bin, due to us making a hash of it. As he enjoyed the feeling of power, being able to humiliate an individual, he thought he had power over us all, what he did not appreciate was the fact that we all sympathised with each other and could not wait for him to get his comeuppance.

He finally got it when he decided, as he was riding on a high unchallenged and enjoying the power of humiliating his chosen subject, to go into unknown territory and push two boys' heads into the bin, together.

We were as part of the lesson, given the task of producing a clay model of any animal or bird of our choice. I chose an eagle and thought it looked very life like, so you can imagine my disappointment when I was accused of not following the brief, I dared to argue with him when he said it looked like an aeroplane, Joe backed me up and said he thought it looked good, with that bod grabbed both of the clay models through them both into the infamous clay bin, he then grabbed both our arms and pulled us towards the bin, grabbing us by the back of our necks, he began pushing our heads forward. We just stood rigid, and I could feel my anger rising, shit what would happen if I could not control the darkness? Joe saved the day, he glanced sideways at me. Then bod gave one more heave, he pushed with all his might, turning red in the face, then he stopped and began shouting at us.

It was not very pleasant for us, not because we were the least bit afraid, but the massive effort caused him to pant an excessively, which in turn caused us to be engulfed by a cloud of obnoxious fumes. He was not pleased but could not afford to show himself up further, so he sent us back to our desks to a duet of bod, bod, bod, to the tune of a song, to feature later in a comedy sketch in Monty python`s flying circus, titled SPAM. You can still find it on social media, it is fun.

The problem for me was that, strangely enough I enjoyed drama, the acting and singing was a way of being in a fantasy, where you could be something or somebody that was completely different to who you really were.

You already know who was head of drama. Yes, breath of death, his actual name was Mr Gandy.

I had the part of Macbeth in a shortened first act of the Shakespeare classic was to be performed at the end of term show at school. We all had great fun whispering the alternative lines we had made up between us, to some of the other lads, putting them off and into his bad books. I loved the way his cheeks sucked in and pouted out and did a funny little twitch when he was at the end of his tether.

I practiced my lines repeatedly. My favourite part of the whole book was the first scene anyway, with the witches making the predictions of Macbeths demise.

I practiced for ages and took it so seriously. the best part of the scene was where the witches prophesied the fate of Macbeth. We all did very well and were almost flawless in our lines, we even managed to cover up with substitute words that blended in so well they went undetected.

Finally, the evening of the play came at the end of term at Christmas and the hall was full of doating parents and even grandparents. We opened to rapturous applause, and this was even before anyone uttered a word, were we assured complete success?

The curtains went back to reveal the scenery, built by us during our art and woodwork lessons. A cavern with a boiling cauldron in the middle, thanks to the lighting effects, built again by us using red bulbs, red paper strips and a fan. To the sound of thunder in the background, in came the three witches, and each one emptied the contents of a small sack into the cauldron, along with each impeccably delivered speech. Then the famous Double, double toil, and trouble; Fire burn, and cauldron bubble.

This had been surprisingly one of the most difficult parts of the opening speeches, for some reason we all thought the words were. Hubble bubble toil and trouble. But this night, perfection.

Each one of the witches recited their lines word for word. Double, double toil and trouble, Fire burn, and cauldron bubble, word for word twice more, without the slightest hint of a stutter or snigger.

I began to wish that I had not accepted the part of Macbeth so eagerly, I now had to remember the mass of lines that I needed to recite, without knowing what they all meant, but I did it!! All was well, we all called out 'Come high or low; Thyself and office deftly show! I followed with Tell me thou unknown power; - One of the witches followed with He knows thy thought: Hear his speech but say thou nought.

Thank heavens my lines were not following because we were ecstatic with our word for word perfection. The first apparition played by Albert now had his chance of fame and uttered what became the immortal words: -

Macbreath! Macbreath! Macbreath! Beware the breath of death; he did not finish the last words, we all froze.

I will never know to this day how I managed to stifle my laugh and say the final words, Whate`er thou art, for thy good caution, thanks. We all bowed and walked exit stage left.

To our complete disbelief nobody even heard the words, not one flash of acknowledgement of the change in script. Everyone was either, in awe of their young budding Royal Shakespeare prodigies. Or had found the words totally alien. I would doubt that many of them knew the difference between Shakespeare and Dickins.

Chapter 11

Kipper

I know sometimes we could be a little annoying, like in technical drawing class when everyone had to stand up and lean over the drawing board, allowing their backsides to be exposed to the irresistible temptation of plunging the tip of a compass into either cheek. To make it worse the teacher would think they were fooling about and would put them into detention after school.

Like the Basterds we were, we would pick on the weakest candidates, who usually congregated together for safety in numbers. But were weak enough, not to band together, to overpower people like us and teach us a lesson ourselves. This would have stopped us being overconfident in getting away with such behaviour. We got so carried away with the use of our drawing compass that we would even give each other a jab, all be it less aggressive than the ones administered to the pair in front of us. Joe decided that on this occasion with the lack of a target in front of him, he would give me a prick with his compass on my leg.

Unfortunately, as I was taken completely by surprise I jumped up and the compass needle went into my leg the full length of the long spike. The effect on Joe was worse than me, I just pulled it out, Joe fainted. I do not think I have ever let him forget it, not the fact that he had decided to prick me but the fact that he had fainted in front of the whole class.

As with most of the teachers back in our schooldays, they taught more than one subject, of course this ment that some of the elder ones were bad at their second subject. It so happened that the elderly technical drawing teacher, nicknamed kipper, due to his old tie, was also the stand in maths teacher. This year, the final one for some lucky ones, Kipper was our maths teacher. What made it worse was the fact that the normal maths teacher was exceptionally good at explaining the mathematical theories to us, and without boasting my results were around 75%, giving me a position of around third in the class.

Poor old kipper had quite a few annoying habits, but the most prolific was his inability to get anybody's name right, you could understand the odd one or two, like one of the boys whose father was half Italian and blessed him with the name Lanjano., or even Joe whose surname was Rulski. But Smith? you could not make it up.

At the end of the term came the results, we all sat expectantly whilst kipper, glasses on the tip of his nose, eyes straining over the top of the lenses, began reading out the names (translations in the brackets) along with the results, from the top to the bottom in order of marks.

The first mark was given out as forty-five peecent (%), which silenced the whole class, this was followed by forty peecent (%), it was so quiet you could have heard a pin drop. Then came me, announced as usual looking over the rim of his glasses. Pertwee (Perkins) thirty-three peecent (%), followed by Smyth (Smith), thirty peecent (%,) he continued down to Roolinskee (Rulski) ten peecent (%).

Then after a brief silence, he looked up again over the top of his glasses and took a deep breath, followed by err, Laganoo (Lanjano) two peecent (%) and after a moment followed up with, and you only got that because you spelt your name right, no doubt you will be paying a visit to the headmaster. No one could believe it, not that Lanjano only got two percent, that kipper knew how to spell his name correctly but did not know how to say it.

I do not think anyone visited the headmaster's office, and we had a new maths teacher at the start of the final term. This new teacher was the most peculiar man you could think of, as bad as the two old favourites, Digger and Thomas. Digger for his passion, in fact obsession with applying the sole of a gym slipper to the backside of a boy in his book's cupboard, and Thomas, better known as chicken whose greatest pleasure was to watch us boys strip off in the cloak room next to the showers and try to whip us with a towel on the cheeks of our backsides with the justification that we were wasting time chattering to arrive late at our next lesson. In our schooldays the normal way of going on.

At the end of the year, Joe left, and I found it incredibly quiet, I missed my old friend. Life still went on and I continued with my studies hoping to get into dockyard and start earning money.

There was a particular six form boy who I detested, he didn`t pick on me particularly, but just targeted our year group. One day he was pushing the younger boys around the playground and as I walked past, he slapped me around the head. It was not even particularly hard, just a sort of statement, I can do anything I want to, you are just a piece of shit type slap.

This was when the blackness returned without any warning at all, Usually I began to feel hot and uncomfortable but this time it descended instantly and the next thing I knew, I had punched him in the face. Being the bigger of the two of us he began punching me as hard as he could. I am afraid he got the better of me, so I was pleased when we were split up by a teacher.

Both of us received two cuts of the cane on both hands. As we walked away, he said that he would see me in the morning and teach me another lesson.

Morning came and I arrived at the school playground I noticed that he and his group of friends were standing obviously waiting for me to arrive. My first instinct was to walk away as fast as possible without drawing any attention to myself, but a voice inside my head kept saying, no teach him a lesson, otherwise he will bully you, you can take him out the more pain you get the less it will hurt as you go on. I walked straight up to him, as he had his back to me at the time, I tapped him on the shoulder and as he turned, I hit him as hard as I could in the face.

He took four or five steps backwards, everybody parted and as he came at me, So I just hit him as hard as I could, but he was still standing, and I was being, hit back. The strange thing was I didn`t feel any pain this time. We fought for 3 minutes before the teacher found us. We were then parted and received another two cuts of the cane each.

The next morning at breaktime, feeling amazed that I had felt no pain, even when I got home and sat down, in fact even my hand showed no sign of the cut of the cane, that usually remained bruised for at least two days. So, I decided that this time I would go looking for the bullyboy, I quite enjoyed the excitement of the pain and as I approached him, he said. 'Look don't let`s fight you can join our gang, we have discussed it, and all agree, even if you are younger than us.' I just held out my hand, kept my eyes fixed on his and said, 'I do not want to join your gang, but I prefer not to get the cane every day. He shook my hand and said 'agreed.'

I had proven to myself that I could stand alone against a bully much like my father and walk away on my terms not his.

Even though School was not easy, it was not the school lessons, just the control. In fact, the lessons came extremely easy to me and some of my best times were at school, we had a lot of fun in some of the lessons, science/biology being one.

Chapter 12

Dog jaw

The school master who taught us science and technology, was a large man who we thought had a speech impediment, it turned out he was born almost deaf, in later years I realised that he was a clever man who had overcome his disability and should have been respected by us all, but back then it was funny to a bunch of teenage boys, that he sounded like a dog barking, especially when he was in a cupboard getting supplies whilst talking to the class.

Hence the nickname he got, dog jaw. We had many an adventure with our biology lessens, we even made a dead frog's leg move with a battery and grew crystals in a test tube, and one of dog jaw`s pride and joys was his tropical aquarium.

He had all sorts of fish, but his favourites were two red fin sharks, they were only small but shaped like a miniature shark. On this day he chose two of us to clean out the aquarium myself being one of them.

The instructions were specific. The second aquarium had been pre-cleaned and heated to the precise temperature needed. We had a small net each and shown exactly how to gently catch the small guppies and other assorted fish and the precise way to catch and transfer the two red fin sharks without causing them any stress.

Trying to net the small guppies was difficult, boring and no fun at all, so we decided it would be easier and much more fun to create a syphon using a piece of clear tubing, as this had been taught us in our science class, we assumed it was an acceptable method to use, we were keeping the fish in water during the transfer, it was only a small amount of water going into the clean tank and the fish would be less stressed. We would hold the end of the tube until we isolated the fish we wanted to transfer, then rapid transfer. It gave us great satisfaction to see them sucked into the tube and blasted into the second tank sitting on a lower table.

All was going well and very efficiently, until as was inevitable, we had emptied all the secondary fish into the second tank, leaving only the red fin sharks.

This is the point where clever inventiveness becomes replaced with sheer stupidity. One of the red fin sharks decided to explore the path taken by its smaller comrades. Instead of quickly covering the end of the tube with the ready poised thumb, so preventing access to the red fin shark. I can boast by the way that it was not me on this occasion.

My co-worker decided it would be an opportunity to reduce our efforts by allowing the beautiful red fin shark to use the interstellar transportation passage. It got halfway up the tube before it stuck fast, there was a blind panic and without any thought we tried blowing up the tube, which did nothing but jam it in even tighter. To make it far worse a smaller tube had been pushed into the first one, which resulted in the destruction of the red fin shark. What could we do absolutely nothing, so we flushed the parts of the fish down the sink and continued with the transfer of the surviving one using the net, this concluded the successful transfer of the second red fin shark, in half the time taken to destroy the first one.

Because of the various plastic modules, such as tunnels and shells in the second tank and the addition of more from the first tank, it was not clear that there was only one red fin shark. Thank heavens that they usually only come together rarely. We were not sure if we got away totally without suspicion and later after the second incident I am about to recall, the intensity of the caning suggested that the suspicion had been there for a while.

Incident two once again, came from an assignment to a practical lesson, this time in learning how to manage a greenhouse, which of course included the complete re-organisation and cleaning of all the shelves, old plant pots and the emptying of the large water container.

We began very diligently, placing all the pot plants on one shelf whilst we cleaned the vacated shelf. Unfortunately, this became a boring mundane job, not fit for such bright students with an extremely low concentration.

So, we decided to introduce the excitement of developing the skill of throwing potted plants across the greenhouse, to the person placing them on the newly prepared shelves.

The extra skill of rotating the plant in its pot during the throw, was introduced to add excitement, the new skill was a complete success, until that is, we reached the cacti plants. This required a whole new level of concentration and handling skills.

The first plant span so that the spikes imbedded themselves in the catcher's hand, which ment he dropped the whole plant and pot onto the tiled floor area, smashing the pot and releasing the potting media. Mild panic set in and instead of re-potting the cacti in a new plant pot, all the debris was thrown into the water tank, including the cactus plant.

The water became black, but we did not notice that all the evidence of our mishandling of the plants, disappeared as if by magic. A new game with its demanding skills had been created, much to everyone's pleasure, it even had a name 'spin the cacti.' This was a brilliant concept, a competition, leaving behind no trace of failure.

Just as we had completed the last spin, and mastered the skills needed to throw, catch, and stack the shelves with dog jaws precious and rare cacti plants, we got the message that he was on the way to approve our practical work lesson.

We all stood immensely proud because, to us the greenhouse looked transformed from an untidy area into a neat clean workplace worthy of any Royal Horticultural Society worker. The plants looked as though they had been professionally spaced out to display their beauty, almost inviting a photograph to send to the local paper.

We all felt proud when his first words were. 'Well done boys this looks very neat and tidy, but you haven't finished, you and you' he said pointing at myself and one of the other lads, 'empty out the water tank, which can't be used on the plants we don't know what is in it.'

I can only describe the feeling as, like blowing up a balloon, when you get to the full size, for some reason you feel compelled to have one last blow, which is when the balloon bursts and all your efforts become meaningless.

We did not dare to argue, so we carried the tank outside, hoping he would stay behind and admire the displays immaculately presented. No chance, we were followed closely by dog jaw, he was being very impatient, tip it out he repeated three times, as if he had psychic powers. No that was not the case at all. He had just far more knowledge of the workings of schoolchildren when put in groups to complete a task they had no interest in. Coupled with being in possession of far more intelligence than we gave him credit for.

Why did not such highly intellectual beings even consider for one moment that a complete pigsty packed with every conceivable plant and weed could transform into a clean and tidy greenhouse, with not a sign of rubbish to dispose of. What idiots it was all too clean, not even a black plastic bag in view. He knew we were too lazy to put the dirt and weeds into the plastic bags, let alone take them to the school tip yards away, like idiots we thought, if we shoved them under our jackets, we could take them home to our mums to use. Oh, if it had been that simple to fool him.

As we tipped the tank over his smug delighted face turned into a fierce bulldog expression, his eyes almost red with rage, even he had not expected the scale of the number of his precious cacti plants that did not make the shelves, all tumbling to the grass along with the debris he was expecting.

This episode taught us a second lesson, one everyone in our class never forgot. Dog jaws massive hands were far more effective as weapons than the modest cane. The thing that stayed with me the most was how a man as big and powerful could have so much love of nature and how cruel we were to not realise the sensitivity of him. Never judge a book by its cover, is the expression I believe.

Chapter 13

Min

Running alongside our excursions into the world of the famous like David Attenborough and David Bellamy. We had been found a new maths teacher, one that was easy to understand, and I learned a lot from. Unfortunately, he was not an extraordinarily strong character, to begin with he was, let say obviously middle class and he resembled a character from a show of our time called, the goon Show, and the character was the husband of Min, who in turn had a voice identical to our new teacher. His name was Crouther.

His biggest problems were, he detested lateness and incorrect precise speech, we were all dominantly Chatham and the surrounding area, with speech I guess you could define as lazy cockney. As an example, we had a practical maths lesson on one day a week, this was building geometric shapes to get us to understand angles and shapes of things like triangles, octagons, and dodecahedrons. A brilliant idea, the problem was, on the second lesson, two things happened to transform the potentially popular lessons. Firstly, one of the less gifted boys arrived late for the lesson, we were already cutting up the card to begin forming a shape. The door burst open and as he entered, he was, rather than apologising, shouting out, 'Av we got practical t`day?' With that he pushed the door closed which made a loud bang.

We all instinctively looked at Min, he was bright red, his eyes were bulging, and his cheeks were both twitching together, something I had never seen before. He completely lost it, he screamed at the top of his voice 'get out you, thick stupid ignoramus.' the youth turned and grabbed the door handle and luckily it opened first time, as he was thrust through the opening with Min pushing him up the corridor by the back of his neck.

We sat in silence, I think every one of us would have been on the side of Min had he sent the boy home, or any other action than the ones he thought were right, bearing in mind we were now heading towards adulthood. Back they both came with Min bringing up the rear carrying the cane. They both stood behind the desk and Min delivered his speech. Now I reflect on it, the only one he could have made, as he was still almost shaking with rage and still bright red.

'Put your hand out you, despicable piece of rubbish,' the youth was trembling. He raised the cane and brought it down on his hand. As most of us had been caned, by at least one of the teachers, our badge of honour was to keep our hand still and not shed a single tear. The youth had no chance, he was terrified and burst into tears. Min then looked at us all and said, 'The next boy who slams my door or talks like a gutter snipe will get this. Hand out boy he shouted, the same one,' both cheeks trembling still, with rage. The youth was trembling as he held out his hand, we could see the red weald across the palm of his hand. This was the moment Min lost us all as he brought the cane down in the same place the first one had landed.

The boy as stupid as he was, it was just him, he was all noise and acted the way he did because he knew he was lacking, that is why he was, held back for an extra year, to try to get him to a level, that he could get some sort of job. In our day there were not the many categories of reasons why someone was, as we defined it, over the top or thick.

We worked through that morning in complete silence, and without showing any reaction to the incident. At lunch we all decided that we would have our protest at the next maths lesson. We drew lots to see who the chosen three were going to be, they would then arrive late for the lesson in order. The first one would only be a minute late and would burst in, importantly closing the door quietly. He would then say the words 'Av we got practical t`day?' The second boy would arrive a minute later taking the exact same action including the words 'Av we got practical t`day?'

I volunteered to be the third and last in line, it was decided on the basis that I had been caned on a few occasions and had been lucky every time that the cane landed around the calluses on my hand, formed by demanding work with Joe's dad on the building sites, so no tears and it was important to show Min that he could not rule us with fear. I conducted the third ritual and Mins' face was red cheeks pulsating, but he sent me to get the cane from the headmaster's office, rather than dragging me there and the cane was not applied, with anything like the ferocity of the earlier administration. No tears, in fact I managed to show no emotion at all and took the cane back to the headmaster's office. It was like an unspoken truce.

Having been through the discipline of caning, did I think it effective? I am unsure, but the way things have progressed, and the result of that progression have not made any noticeable difference and in fact the whole fabric of democracy hangs by a fine thread in this now dictatorial phase of political evolution. But we should save this topic until the end, when there can be a direct comparison between the past and the future, (to become the present by the conclusion of this story).

It was the last week of the end of summer term and I along with the rest of our fifth year class were leaving school, I had already taken an examination for entry to the dockyard and come surprisingly high in the order, allowing me to choose whichever profession I wanted, the number one profession being electrical fitter in HM dockyard, so I decided this was what I would do, to allow me to earn my own money, rather than earn a pittance at the shop cutting up carcasses. Although sometimes I could dream, I was cutting up my old man, as I now referred to him.

I considered the word Father afforded him too much respect. Things would be a lot better as I was starting to get older and more sensible and had not actually experienced any of the dark side as I called it, for a long time, but it was never far away.

The final year at school began with the sudden resurgence of my darker side, maybe because Joe wasn`t there so I missed the fun we had, or I had just begun to grow into an adult with all the associated feelings and simply became more serious. Unfortunately, most of the lads we had upset, were the ones that stayed on at school to sit the exams. So thought they would teach me a lesson and make my life a little more unbearable, but I did not care I no longer feared anything physical.

This, our leaving day, prompted a few boys in the fourth year, to believed it would be nice to upset the fifth-year leavers, mainly because these little shits as we called them believed we were boffs, who deserved humiliation, before they left a week later.

This humiliation to be conducted in front of the girl's school playground.

These lads of course did not know many of us but thought safety in numbers would assure success and that six to one was reasonable odds to ensure they indeed succeeded in their quest.

To make it even easier for them, we left the classroom at separate times to come out to the playground as we were getting all our classwork presented to us, so this ensured isolation for periods of time.

I do not know what had happened before I left the classroom, but I was surprised to see so many girls giggling in their play area just opposite to ours, but I was about to find out.

The obvious leader of the pack of boys came towards me flanked by two others. I stopped in front of them, and the lead boy said, 'OK mate drop your trousers.

I of course laughed.

'I mean it he said, get them off or we will take them off for you pants as well.' The girls the same age group as the boys, began chanting, off, off, off. I began to feel strange, fear of humiliation. 'We will hammer the shit out of you if you don't' he said. I answered with the first thing that came into my head, which was. 'You probably will eventually, but at least you'll never see again.'

He just stared at me; I heard the voice in the distance which I knew was my own, although I did not seem to be in control of the words I was saying. 'I'll blind you and your mate before I go down.' I felt so calm and showed not one bit of emotion, just the way I was when my father used to be laughing at me as I was degraded, into little more than an object, to show the power the bitch he was using could have over me, if I were not strong enough.

Obviously, the boys decided it was better not to see how capable I was in conducting my threat, and decided that it was better to back off, so they turned away and the leader made some comment under his breath, which I happily ignored.

There was a moment of complete silence, one of the girls, quite attractive, smiled at me and said, 'what would you have done? I replied without even thinking, 'how do I know they decided their eyes are the softest part of their body and one of their biggest assets in life, so if they wanted to keep them, they needed to back off.' She looked as though she did not even understand what I had said and replied, 'I have got other useful assets apart from my eyes, if you are interested in finding them.'

After the intensity of emotion, I had just experienced, her body was the farthest from my mind, although I at once assumed that was her meaning, it could have been she had discovered the meaning of life, but I doubt it. Strangely enough I did meet her later which features in my story, it was a very brief one but quite amusing.

My true love was to come much later when I was

able to control the dark side with the help of her love.

Chapter 14

The dark side

Strangely enough much later than this period in my life, a space series called Star Wars, was released into the cinemas and the writer had called the evil side of the battle for supremacy, the dark side, I had already coined this phrase, I wonder why he had chosen it as well.

I had to control my emotions especially the anger I held inside. I had many encounters with my father and to write about them all, would be boring and repetitious. So, I will keep them to a minimum and jump forward to Christmas 1967, that is when it first started to come to a dangerous head between us both. He was so petty, he could come home at any time and demand his food, but if he decided he wanted us all to eat together, that is what had to happen.

He always needed to be in complete control, just a simple example of the depth of his pettiness. We all loved our mother's cottage pie, for those who have not had one, it is simply beef mince, onion, peas, and gravy topped with mash potatoes and baked in the oven.

According to him he hated it, and my mother was not allowed to make it when he ate with us. However, the thick idiot loved mince and mash potato. With fried onion and peas on the side. How could you even begin to understand the brain of an imbecile like that.

I asked my mother if for this once, I could miss Christmas dinner and eat it later in the day, as Joe and I were invited to a Christmas party at one of our mutual friends' houses.

My mother of course said yes and added 'but don't be too late back.' As this was just an afternoon party and his parents were both present, I knew this would not go on too long, so I replied yes, no problem I'll be back around 7pm.

With that I left the house and met up with Joe. We had an enjoyable time and had a few drinks, there was not enough alcohol to have any effect on me and anyway I had enough drinks from the age of fourteen to be sure that I could never noticeably get drunk.

I got a lift back from the party and after dropping people off at various places, got back home at around 7.30 pm. I opened the back door and entered the kitchen. There I was confronted by my father in a rage shouting obscenity whilst moving threateningly towards me. That same darkness descended on me, it is so difficult to describe because it is like I am in a dream, everything is in slow motion even the visible movements of the people around me, everything other than the object of my attention is black. It is like all my concentration is on the focal point. At the worst I just seem to have not even been there, what I see is the devastation left. I could hear myself saying 'back off you piece of shit, touch me and it's the last thing you will ever do.' At the same time, I instinctively backed up to the sink and grabbed a milk bottle, they were all made of glass back then.

I smashed it into the sink holding the neck of the bottle and brought it up towards his face. He instantly backed up, I moved forward, causing him to back up even farther. His next words were 'so you think you are a big man with that in your hand.' Something inside me told me now is the time, you can kill him now, no more pain. I do not know why but I was not completely in darkness, but all I could see was the fear in his eyes.

At that very moment, my mother came into the dining room, her face full of terror. At that instant everything became reality. Then came that reality. I could never win by plunging the bottle into his neck. If he died, I would spend a long time in prison, just to destroy an arsehole. Mum would be alone with no money because he had gambled that all away.

If he didn`t die, I could never live there any longer with him and would lose my family. Never once did I consider the possibility that he could have killed me, for some reason I never even thought of being defeated, I had enough of that. Never again will I be afraid of anything or anyone. This was the turning point, I had been to the darkest place, I thought.

I was at last beginning to be able to control the anger and by channelling the hatred through my eyes and body motions, I could almost make people think twice about their actions.

On this occasion, more by luck than conscious actions, he decided not to go for me at once, this cut through the tension, and I could see my mother was between us. I had time to calmly turn around, walk to the sink and smash the bottle into the sink and saying, 'I don't need this.'

By now my mother was between us and gave him the out he needed, she said 'I told Keith he could stop out and he came back not too late as I asked him, so leave him alone.' It was the first time she had really gone against him, and the result was, he turned and disappeared up to their bedroom and remained there for the rest of the night.

I kept asking in my head for my guardian as I called the apparition, to destroy him and not allow him to be part of my life for too much longer. Like every incident in life the importance of it diminishes and the incident becomes a distant thing that has no real substance as life goes on.

This incident however at the time, proved to me that I had to do something drastic to control my pent-up anger and walk away from confrontational situations as much as I could. I was not mad, was I? had I damaged myself for ever? Will I always have to be alone. It sounds so dramatic, but it was real, back then.

I realised I was not in full control of my actions and needed to wait before I reacted. As time progressed, I realised this was one of the hardest things for me to achieve. Making the right choice for each individual incident I would face. Sometimes I would get it right, but the times I got it wrong, both the decision to react or to back off, stayed with me for a long time.

Most times I regretted not just reacting, because then it was too late and all you had to do was face the consequences, of your action and not weather you were right or wrong to take that action. This made me consider the consequences of my hesitation, as I reconsidered repeatedly if my choice was the right one.

Since my Christmas incident however all had been quiet at home and the old man had decided not to chance another confrontation.

The odd thing was, soon after the confrontation, he developed what is known as a carbuncle. A massive poisonous spot that goes into the body rather than bursts out like a normal spot.

This was revolting and no doubt painful, like the

description of its host. The more he screamed as my mother tried to clean and re-dress it, the more I enjoyed his anguish. But I still had not had my ultimate revenge, that had yet to come.

I was lucky because learning came quite easy to me and I was lucky to have a good memory, which helped with exams. The art was not trying to understand everything as taught to you, just remember the key formulars in maths and science, dates of events in history and where countries were in the world, their time zones, and contours for geography.

I am sure this approach got me good levels in my GCSE`s and I came high in the exams set to enter the Dockyard at Chatham in Kent. This resulted in me having the choice of any of the trades offered.

I finally decided on being an electrical fitter and secured a four-year apprenticeship and a chance to gain the relevant technical qualifications, through the local college, all free of charge, it meant that my love of art had to take second place, which was a shame but became a source of immense pleasure in later years.

It felt like a new phase in my life, but I did not understand what the transmission from a child to an adult really meant. The unfortunate thing was that the transition was not stark, I was not a child one minute and an adult the next, I had no more, not even different experiences of life, in the beginning, you had the weak boys and the bullies, they were just older. Having said all this, it was an interesting part of my journey of life. We were based at the training college at Chatham naval base, at that period there were no female electrical apprentices, so we were an all-male intake, the only women in the facility were the cleaners.

Chapter 15

Fly me to the moon

In this period of time, science and instrumentation was advancing rapidly, and the Americans planned to launch Appollo1 into orbit. Onboard were Gus Grissom, Roger Chaffee, and Ed White.

During the final test stages prior to lift off, a fire erupted and all three were killed, so bad was the incident that it was reported that, all three were fused to the interior of the cabin, all of them died of asphyxiation.

This of course was a massive setback to the planned Moon landing, which was to boost the Technology of space travel beyond the reach of Russia. This being the case there were a large amount of European scientist and experts in the programme, Irish and English personnel making up many of the numbers on the space projects. There was an outcry to abort the space programme, due to the risk of human lives.

There was, of course, never a possibility of abandoning the space programme, the whole of the so-called free world countries were involved. So, democracy being ignored. 21st July 1969 Apollo 11 was Launched and along with the first man to walk on the moon, put America ahead of the world of Technological achievements.

After this Apollo's 12,14,15,16 and 17made moon landings with astronauts, meaning six flags are still on the moon. Ironically, Apollo 13 mission had to be aborted due to an explosion of an oxygen tank, but the technical achievements of the scientists were proven sound, when it was returned safely to Earth.

So, my generation had seen space travel for real. In fact, it was now old hat and Apollo 17 was the last landing. Everyone had lost interest unless it was going to lead to greater space travel advancements.

Unfortunately, as it turned out the technological advancements due to the spin offs from the space programme, had given rise to advancements in photography, and illusionary lifelike games, so advanced that by 2022 the football players in a game's software appear to be actual people.

I say unfortunately because later on, the latest craze, was to be questioning the achievements of those early years, using the very source of the spectacular technology developed, because of those years.

Did we old farts believe we landed on Mars? No that was clearly an April fool's day hoax. There was no proof of our technological advances ever giving us the ability to travel at even half the speed of light. If there had of been then we could have done the distance it in about an Hour.

Do we believe man walked on the moon? Well apparently, around 75% did, at the time, me being one of them, and still do.

Now with Artificial Intelligence, maybe I had taken the right path in eventually choosing technology over creativity, art, or house building. Maybe I did have something to thank my father for after all?

Chapter 16

Simple Cyril says

Back to my apprenticeship, because as I mentioned previously, it was an all-male environment and three-year groups. The alpha male syndrome was ever present. Of course, we the newbies, were fair game and had to endure being locked in the mock submarine, bursting for a pee. This was a wooden replica of a submarine hull, fitted out with instrumentation, and we had to run cables to the various instruments and connect them up, so that they could develop our ability.

This was where I got my first experience of a 650 Volt shock, which only threw me across the floor, no side effects but as there were only two witnesses and we never reported the incident, it did not have a much significant meaning. Until a little later in the month.

One of the favourite pranks amongst the older

apprentices, was to wire up a hand voltage generator known as a megger, turning the handle fast gave the person touching the ends of the two cables a high voltage shock, not enough to electrocute them, but enough to give them considerable pain.

The favoured way of administrating the shock was to connect one electrode to the metal bench and bury the other electrode into a container full of metal bolts. They would then wait until someone had their hand on the metal bench top and reached into the container to retrieve a metal bolt. I must confess I was caught by this, the first time I jumped with surprise, which gave the second-year guys a laugh. However, the second time it happened to me I was ready, holding my hand in the box while the idiot frantically turned the handle, gave me immense pleasure.

This was especially pleasing, when his extremely thick partner in crime, thought the instruments battery had run out and threw it onto the floor at the same time as the instructor entered the workshop. He got the usual punishment of hand sawing twenty pieces of metal bar after the end of the day's work. No one knew, including me that my tolerance to voltage shocks at low current was excellent.

I made a few friends at the college but kept myself to myself, this suited me as I was not particularly in need of company, I much preferred my own. This meant that people did not really know me and hence kept a friendly distance most of the time. We progressed to the second year and became the older boys. Strangely the new intake was full of loud bullyboys who were, as we called them 'up their own arses.' In the beginning some of their antics were extremely funny and this increased their bravado.

The incident I found most amusing was when one of the instructors, who we all knew was having sex with one of the women cleaners, using the mock-up of the submarine during our lunch hour. This time he found himself locked in the submarine with the cleaner, courtesy of a first-year apprentice. They were only released at clocking out time, to the loud clapping and cheering of every apprentice. They had been given their freedom, by the timekeeper whose name was Cyril.

I mention Cyril to bring in another of my favourite entertainments, dreamt up by the latest intake of apprentices. Cyril was around mid-forties and a little slow, not stupid but easily wound up, sometimes almost causing him to hyper-ventilate.

The procedure went as follows. The first boy would put his card into the machine and push down the handle, which worked the punch system recording the time. He pushed down so hard that the whole clock unit shook on the wall, this action, repeated by each apprentice, until Cyril broke into a rage shouting out stop!!! Whilst turning almost purple. With this the whole ensemble of apprentices clocking in would sing at the top of their voices, the Cyril song, to the music of the simple Simon says, ditty.

Simple Cyril says don't bang the clock cos you'll knock the fucker off the wall.

Simple Cyril says if you do it again, I'll come over and fuck you all.

After repeating these lines over about three or four times, Cyril would be bright red with rage and invariably the instructors would arrive in force and discipline the few boys at the front of the que. This would manifest in the sawing up of solid bars of metal for an hour after home time. You can imagine the chaos as everyone scrabbled to ensure they were not at the front of the que.

I seemed to end up with a lot of sawing bar's, not that I was rebellious and always in trouble, just unlucky. We discovered that an impressive weapon, using a piece of metal conduit pipe and a ball of sealing compound, made to the exact dimensions as the internal diameter of the pipe could be made. The distance that the ball could travel from the pipe became an event taken as seriously as the records achieved in the Olympics.

Every electrical apprentice had his blowpipe and compound and at breaktime, small groups (to avoid detection by the instructors), gathered at the open windows to try to break the existing distances achieved by the current record holder. On this occasion I had scientifically worked out the best diameter and length of pipe, coupled with the diameter of the compound encasing a small ball bearing to add weight to the flight. I took a deep breath and blasted the compound through the tube. The result was astounding, in fact the ball crossed the entire distance between the buildings and smashed through the window opposite, which happened to be the office of the head teacher at the college. Luckily, he was not in the office, unluckily the noise of cheering and laughter caught the attention of the instructors, resulting in double punishment and the cost of a replacement glass windowpane.

Still my main problem was lack of control over whatever it was inside that took over when I felt threatened physically or emotionally. There were occasions where it was an asset, then others that caused all sorts of problems including threat of expulsion from the college. I would of course argue that it was never of my making, but I have later realised my reactions were in the extreme. As this story goes on you will, I am sure, make your own judgments on the incidents.

The straightforward process of living through adolescent to adulthood comes with constant incidents, ones imposed on you, ones you must meet because of others, ones you choose to take and ones that just happen because of circumstances beyond everyone's control.

The ones imposed on me were in my early years and of course, shaped the reactions to all the other incidents that followed. Much later in this story, we get to the up-to-date situations, at that stage it goes full circle and things imposed on us all cause reactions that have been designed to divide and conquer us even as citizens of our country of birth,

No one is absolutely free in any Country and the protection of citizens is just a pipedream to keep control.

One incident that happened, helped me to concentrate on trying to control my actions rather than be controlled by them. It was a simple thing coming out of a combination of random incidents that would have been prevented easily, with just a bit of thought.

It happened during a project test piece, where a cube of metal had to be able to pass through a cut-out in a second piece of metal in all rotations of the cube.

I had filed the cube of metal and was on a drilling machine trying to drill a series of holes in the second metal plate to file out the four sides, leaving a square through which the cube would pass in all directions. There was a person waiting to use the drill after me, but I was obviously not quick enough for him, so being in the year higher than me he decided he would physically remove me from the drill to allow him to take over. As he pulled me off, the metal plate spun around and cut into my hand. He at once let go of me, obviously he had not intended for me to get hurt. It would however been better if he had not made that decision, as I did not remember what happened next, other than a rage as great as the time I was attacked outside the dance hall.

My next recollection was my removal by a group of people from the person who attacked me, he was unconscious and covered in blood and vomit. It happened that it had taken three instructors to pull me of the person and calm me down. He went to the surgery and then sent home for the day.

I came close to losing my apprenticeship and only spared that humiliation, by the very same person at the end of my rage, taking full responsibility for the cause of my attack. We shook hands and the incident was closed, but for me it showed that my decisions were not controlled, as I had thought, and I had to somehow control my anger without losing the edge if I needed it.

I made a pact with myself that I would control my actions by understanding myself. This, as crazy as it seems, was talking to my inner self and understand how to control my flashes of extreme anger. Believe me much harder to achieve than talk about but has brought many benefits later to my life.

The second related incident happened not long after, I decided to take up boxing and was doing very well, the only problem was, whereas it helped me control of my anger, I did not like being hit, and had to concentrate to retain control when I got hurt, knowing that losing control meant I felt no pain it was easier to give up control to anger. Then came the incident that changed a lot in me and showed me that gaining time to form a strategy allowed me to control my actions.

It started at one of our breaktimes, being young and sheeplike, we all smoked cigarettes even though as apprentices we could not really afford them. This of course meant the bully boys liked to, as they termed it, 'bum a ciggy', another way of saying steal a cigarette.

This day, the usual three, the bullyboy and his two sidekicks, came around to random people and grabbed their cigarette packets with the famous words 'gis a fag.' As they got to me, I covered the packet with my hand, to which he made his next mistake and threatened. 'Right down the bogs' Which, in words used by someone with a bit of intelligence would have been, come down to the toilets and we will beat you up for not giving us your cigarettes.

This I had decided would now be the test of my newly practiced, 'controlled aggression. Never act on impulse, assess the situation, look for the quickest way to win with the least aggression but with maximum, wipe-out.

He confidently strolled in front like an inflated prick towards the toilet block, I was directly behind him and his henchmen behind me that was his first mistake, boxed in and nowhere to manoeuvre, perfect for me. As he opened the twin doors like a western gunslinger and the two henchmen dashed to the side of me to catch and hold open the doors, the sinks were directly in front of us, the doors held, one by each of the henchmen, ready to close them to hide my beating, from any passing instructor.

I simply made three quick strides building up momentum grabbed one shoulder and the back of his head, which I smashed down into the sink, purposely avoiding the dangerous taps, which if I had my usual total anger blackout, would no doubt have caused lasting damage to his face.

He dropped like a stone to his knees, I turned and without raising my voice or looking at his slumped body, said, 'who's next?' They stood, still holding the doors open, so I simply walked out and back to my desk.

All of us learnt a lesson that day. Them to be aware of their failings and not to assume everyone reacts the same and fears violence.

For me at last, controlled aggression is far less dangerously unpredictable than pure rage, and far more effective. Gaining the time to walk to the toilet block took away the need to react dangerously. It is strange but many years later one of my own sons, through anger during a petty disagreement, said the same words and offered me to go outside to assumably settle the disagreement through the result of a fight. Or hopefully just to see if I would back down, seems like the young lion trying to take over as the head of the pride.

He strutted in front of me heading for the front door, I could almost see the sinks replacing the front door. Fortunately, my eldest son stood between us and diffused the situation. I was pleased because glass is far more unpredictable than solid porcelain.

I gave up boxing, purely because I knew I would never master full control of my aggression and I needed some of the adrenalin that came with the rage to reduce the pain, weird but true, if I was hurt the pain became extra strength.

Much later I, started judo and found that this helped even more with my ability to think before acting and in fact the perfect throw, came when the timing of an action was perfect, using the aggression of the opponent to aid the throw, and not just pure aggression from me.

A good friend of mine was later to teach me a second form of martial art, Aikido which again uses the opponent's aggression against them. Far more dangerous in its basic form and far more difficult to control the timing, to limit the damage to the opponent. I enjoyed it because you were totally in control of how much pain you caused to the opposition, just by the positioning of their limb, or the speed of the action. This was proven when we were out with a friend having a drink, he wasn't into martial arts as it is known, he was a tough Liverpudlian who thought he was too tough to need special training. We got into a slightly heated discussion, and it ended with our friend stating that he could take my mate Dave out any time, Dave replied 'of course you can if you come up behind me in the back of the neck without me having any inclination of a remote possibility of that happening but give me one second to react and you will lose.'

He then smugly said one and through a punch at Dave. I must admit it happened so quickly I didn't have time to see the action that resulted in our mutual friend lying on the floor with his arm positioned in such a way that a slight movement would have resulted in it being broken. Suffice to say the mutual friend learnt a lesson to remember.

I learnt a lot from our practice sessions and Dave was very quick to learn the Judo moves, I could never move with the speed he had, but then he had started at six years old, the lesson I learnt was there is always someone better or faster than you, so you also have to gain enough time to slow the opposition down by some means and never be certain that you will win, there will always be someone better. This goes for anything in life.

Chapter 17

Manhood, really?

Ok now we get past the boyhood stage and into the most exciting part of life. The progression into adulthood.

I was now going to further education classes and mixing with new people although Joe was still my best friend and as it happens still is and will be until the day one of us dies.

As our lives took different paths, we both had other friends that we did not share due to our different lives, although one of Joe's friends became my brother-in-law.

Having said this, we usually went out to the dance venues, trying to meet girls, to enhance our lives. Think back to the playground when I was targeted as one of the guys to suffer the humiliation of, being stripped in front of the girls.

Well, the girl in question had risen to the level of

having most of the young studs after her for a date and other things, which she apparently hinted at, but never confirmed or denied. However, the result of the uncertain outcome of an encounter brought her many admirers' offering free drinks just on the slim chance the boasts by her suitors were true. Remembering her last comments to me, I decided to chance my arm, encouraged by Joe of course.

After her greeting me with a very sexy smile and look of good things to come, the next words to leave her mouth were 'are you going to buy me a drink?' I was expecting this, the usual standard chat. Yes, I replied, and she held my arm as we walked towards the bar. 'What would you like' I asked, expecting the usual reply from the more level-headed girls babysham or cherry B?' Her reply was Brandy and babysham. I was devastated as this was the equivalent of a day's pay, but with my newfound coolness, I ordered it and a pint of beer for myself. The bartender put down the drinks on the bar, I picked up my pint and walking away said she`s paying. I winked at her and said thanks for that. I do not know what happened at that stage as I disappeared into the throngs of sweaty youths to enjoy my free pint. No not one reprisal, but there was something just waiting to teach me a lesson in humility.

The next dance was at the same venue, Joe and I were meeting two girls we were interested in, and everything was progressing well as we all four sat in the corner drinking. Unfortunately, Joe and I had been drinking at his home and had around four pints each before we left to go to the venue.

I looked across at Joe and even in the darkness of our dimly lit corner seats, I could see his face becoming paler. Then without warning he was sick, sending a projectile of vomit over both the girls and me. I must admit the few seconds warning I had gained ment I got off with only a small splash. With that he collapsed onto the floor, I apologised to the girls and begged for their forgiveness. Their response was predictable and even though their entire evening was ruined it was obvious any sparks had been completely extinguished. We never did see either of them again.

So, there was Joe completely out of it absolutely covered in his own vomit. I dragged him to the toilets with our mates laughing, two of whom were his elder cousins, they made out he had nothing to do with them. So, I ended up eventually lifting him on to a surface in the gent's toilet, unfortunately this surface was right next to a radiator which only made the situation worse for him.

After a lot of comments from lads who were lining up to use the toilets, I eventually decided to try to get him back to his house. I got him in a fireman's lift, which is supposed to distribute the weight more evenly across the shoulders, I must admit it did not feel that way to me. I started off towards the field that was situated behind his cousin Dina`s place. As we approached the stile to access the field, I felt exhausted, he was just coming around, so I sat him on the top of the stile.

First mistake, he toppled backwards over the stile and landed in a crumpled heap in the field. In one way this was good because it ment I did not need to struggle to get him back onto the stile. The downside was that some way I had to lift him up onto my shoulder again. Well, this would have made a fantastic video post in today's media circles, but then it was just a massive pain in the arse. You can Imagine the rest of the journey down the field, me falling under his dead weight, him bringing up the remaining contents of his stomach, over the grass and my clothes, depending how far he had been launched from my shoulders during the stumble.

Eventually we reached the bottom of the field and only needed to climb up the alleyway to Dina`s place. I decided we should rest there for a while, not because I had made any sensible decision, but just that I was completely exhausted and incapable of going even one step further without Joe being able to at least stumble by the side of me.

I still to this day am pleased that I can consume enormous amounts of alcohol without having much effect, I cannot imagine what would have happened to us both if we had been incapacitated at the same time. As you can imagine Dina was not best pleased to see the state of Joe, but as usual she took care of him like a big sister, and I left him in her capable hands and set off home. Luckily, I did not live extremely far from Joe and Dina, so I sneaked in through the front door and went straight up to the bathroom and cleaned myself up, without anyone knowing the state I had been in.

Fifty-five years later we both still remember the incident, although my version differs in its detail to Joe`s, due to his blank moments. Very few relationships last the length ours will, we really did have it sussed.

As I said before although we were and still are, as close as brothers, like brothers we also had our own lives, which had diversified, our careers went totally in different directions, and I still had my demons of which only a very few were known then and even up to the present by Joe.

I sometimes feel sad that I could never really discuss my true feelings with anyone, even Joe, I suppose it is just that I was not even sure if some of it was just a fantasy. Is there a line between truth and fantasy? Wanting things so much sometimes masks what really is happening, making it almost impossible to separate the two.

I tried so hard to understand myself and never succeeded, it was not that simple. Sometimes there were vivid visions of experiences I knew I was yet to have, coupled with a feeling I was part of another person in another time in the past or future, sometimes momentary confusion when I would read something that I had known months before, was going to happen. It did not seem possible that I was believing I could see into the future, which has got to be, a dream or complete bullshit. So, I kept it all to myself,

Later, as I grew older and became far more experienced, I wrote down my thoughts as they happened and matched them to events that happened later, in other words, what then would have been the future. Sometimes I was somewhere else whilst knowing that could not be the case. There were times when these feelings came over me, I could predict what was going to happen next.

I can now read YOUR thoughts, why didn't I win on the football pools or horse racing, my only answer is simple, if only I knew.

My, let us just call it foresight, showed itself later in my life. It was somehow knowing the thoughts of someone, usually when they were about to cheat me or cause me harm. Nothing that should have been obvious, not a particular look, just an uneasy feeling and a change in tone of the conversation, allowing me to see into their thoughts and question myself why would they say a particular sentence that did not relate to the look they were outwardly showing.

Later, in this story I will elaborate with an incident seen by my business partner, which has remained with him forever, still not having a clue how I knew what was going on, because he was there the entire time and did not notice a single vibe that I later told him of. Even now he still has a problem knowing how my feeling of the meeting, was the total opposite to his.

I had finally accepted that even I, would always struggle to understand and accept what happened in my early life and its perceived effect on my future, sometimes everything seems like a dream, but I always instinctively understand the meaning of the core action being taken, either physically or mentally.

Chapter 18

Big Rachell

So let us continue with the main core of the story, someone reading this account of my life so far will recognise the same type of dilemma presented often.

Although we think we are the only one, and all our experiences and beliefs are unique, this cannot be the case because writers and film makers have elements in their creations that mirror some of the basic elements of my experiences, so what is real and what is fantasy?

Now I had reached a calm acceptance of my inner thoughts and outward actions I was much happier to go out and have fun in groups and leave any aggression to them, my protective instinct was instantaneous and above doubt.

In fact, some of the incidents were a source of entertainment. Back in my day the so-called political correctness was only just manifesting itself. I can remember on one occasion we went out for a drink after college to the local pub, the bartender at this pub was, we called him a queer. I do not even know what we must call him now, it is far beyond my intellectual capability. Sufficient to say, we called him Big Rachell, BR for short.

He was a big youth and wrestled in his spare time, he was a nice person always cheery and joking around. It was just before Christmas, and he was standing on a table putting up decorations. He saw us and shouted out in his normal effected speech 'hello boy's, an echo came back from a group of four Irishmen, we knew they were Irish because of their strong accents. BR ignored them and asked us what we wanted; every time he spoke the four guys mimicked him in a gay voice. Had it been a couple of years earlier I would have made some derogatory comment, but the new me decided to stay silent and watch.

BR continued to ignore them and after he had pulled our pint's he said, 'look after the bar boys, just going for a quick wee.' Off he went towards the toilets, a small deliberation happened between the Irish guys, and they headed towards the toilets as well. My friends had not even been aware of what was happening, so when I said to them 'I think we should go and check on BR' they looked blankly, I then pointed out that the four Irishmen had followed him, and BR could be in trouble. Their reactions were very mixed to say the least and only one stood up to follow me.

I must admit this was the first time my calculated reaction made me feal scared. Just as I reached the gents toilet door it flew open, and BR passed me saying in his usual effected speech 'silly boys will they never learn.' I pushed open the door and inside, two sprawled on the floor and two in one of the open toilets, were the Irishmen, my friend and I looked at each other and turned around back to the bar.

Again, I had learnt a vital lesson. Never judge a book by its cover, this coupled with my newfound, think first before reacting, should have saved me from everything, but I still had to discover how to combine them, or discover yet another element to make that final winning combination in life.

I always blamed the overdose for damaging my brain, but it could not be that simple because it was not only my thoughts that were strange, but my entire day to day feelings were also strange. No headaches, hardly ever sick, able to drink heavily without getting drunk and what became worst of all in later life, resistance to local anaesthetics. Later in the story, I will elaborate on this.

The one thing that happened back in the days of the seance which I have tried many times through my life without any success at all, is to move an object by thought, as had happened once before. It becomes increasingly likely that both me and Joe were wrong about the incident happening, which if it had not been for the written proof of the psalm, the whole supernatural element of this story would not exist.

As I wrote down word for word from a random choice from the whole bible, by Joe and the fact he kept it. Every incident in this story could be just complete fantasy in my head. So why can't I achieve this one act to prove beyond doubt to myself, that everything I know happened, did happen? There is no single act that will ever prove complete certainty of oneself. The elements that existed at that one moment in time. May never be able to be replicated by me.

A Stephen Hawkins quantum moment, or part of the 'spooky' theory by Einstein?

In reality of course all I had remaining; were the consequences of the actions I took as a child. Could I now as a young man rectify or learn to control myself, without the need to blame my actions on my father.

The time of our youth was, like every generation believes an exciting one, entertainment was at the forefront and the latest music styles, instruments and groups were appearing.

Hair styles and clothes were different to the clothes and styles we had as young children, everyone was a clone of their parents in the early post war.

Then as if by magic first the Teddy boys, rock and roll then the Mods, Rockers, and the Flower people. dividing the youth into groups defined by dress, music and even transport choice. The Mods with their scooters and the Rockers with motorbikes. I can remember the first exciting experience of going on a trip organised by one of the fathers of an apprentice in our year group. A trip to the studios of a televised show, called ready steady go. There were a few singers and groups playing live at the show. The main attraction being a group called The Rolling Stones. It was fantastic. I became a lifelong fan after I had met them in a local cinema.

The Rolling Stones, were to perform at our central hall but unbelievably the gig, never happened, due to lack of interest, so they went to the cinema, where we just happened to be waiting to get in. Unfortunately, we were too young to appreciate the situation as they were older than us by a few years, but I could sense the excitement generated by the fact that they were different, carefree, and excitingly rowdy. I am pleased that I took a photograph of them and because of my passion of art. I drew them altogether, they eventually split with Bill Wyman

Five dropped to four with the death of Brian Jones and two members changed. Before the end of this book. Their drummer Charlie Watts also passed away but much later on I am happy to say. I have a drawing of the line-up that lasted until I was old as well. In fact, I went to see them at Edinburgh with my two sons. But more about that further on in the story.

I first saw the original line up on a trip organised by one of the apprentices as I mentioned, his father paid for the journey to the venue, and we only had to pay for the tickets, it was worth every penny. My only disappointment was we were close to the stage and not one of them remembered me from the cinema, they just bloody well ignored me. I don't think my mates believed it had ever happened, I mean who would ever have thrown away their autographs???

We also joined in groups of apprentices to go down to the coast, just to have battles between the Mods and Rockers at a favourite town called Margate. The pop group that was classed as being the music of the Mods was the Beatles, I actually appreciated the music of both groups along with a few other icons. My drawing of those are shown below. Unfortunately, some of those have not survived to this era, John Lennon was shot and killed in New York outside the Dakota building where he lived with Yoko Ono on 8th December1980, the time 11pm.

George Harrison died of the dreaded cancer and Elvis Presley also passed away. I did eventually see both Rod Stewart and Diana Ross live on stage, but that was much later on, in the story.

Getting back to the younger days I can remember on one occasion we all left on a trip to see a new group at the dreamland ballroom Margate, they were called the Equals.

I was on the back of a scooter, wearing an oversized duffle coat, no crash helmet, or gloves and just a pair of jeans with chisel toed shoes (they cost a fortune but were a must have), off we went full of excitement, we travelled about twenty miles when we joined the main road into Margate, it had three main roundabouts. We were travelling at around seventy miles an hour, as we approached the second roundabout there was a truck that clearly entered the roundabout too fast and had Jack knifed across the roundabout, my pal saw it at the last moment and dropped the scooter, both of us hit the ground at high speed, slid under the truck, hit the curb stones of the roundabout, and travelled for a further eight to ten feet. My friend took the skin from his cheek down to the bone, broke his arm and ankle. I got a grass stain on my jeans. The force was with me, Mick still bears the scar on his cheek.

There were a lot of live groups playing at local venues, but of course the entrance fees were quite expensive, especially the ones playing at the good venues like the one I mentioned at the dreamland ballroom, along with needing transportation. If back then, like me you were on an apprentice wage. These trips were exceedingly rare.

We did have a few venues closer to home, one of those was at a place called Rochester Castle. Many of the local up and coming groups played there. But then came along a new scene and source of entertainment. Joe had a leaflet pushed through his letterbox and when I got to his house he said.

'I had this pushed through the door, but I have not got a clue what it is about, it`s a (Dis cove you), I had a look at the leaflet and laughed, it was announcing free entry to a new venue in our area for music and dancing a discotheque. I explained that it was a club where you dance to recordings of pop music. If he ever reads this, I am sure I will be in his bad books for a while but at the time, after calling me something that I would prefer not to print, we had a good laugh and decide we would go along with a few of our mates, one of them being an apprentice bricklayer who was at college with Joe, his name was Colin.

This marked a turning point in both of our lives, as he became my brother-in-law, after we both met our wife's to be, on that fateful night. Colin would have been a mod as he had a scooter. The venue was at the local airport, it was an existing building and was licenced for food and drink. So unfortunately, due to regulations, drinking was allowed only where food was also being consumed.

The answer was quite simple, the door attendants gave everyone entering a paper plate with a piece of cheese and a bread roll on it. Of course, this meant in the corner of the entrance hall was a mountain of discarded food, still an effective way of conforming to the entrance regulations. The government were as astute then, as now.

The main attractions were, the disco music, dancing, and the girls. It had previously been a strip club, then a venue for the little-known local bands, although a couple of these bands did get into the UK charts.

Chapter 19

The black-haired beauty

We had been at the dance for a couple of hours when I noticed this black-haired girl dancing with another girl, who I discovered, later was her younger sister, in fact she had four sisters in total, her being the eldest.

Just as I was about to approach her, I noticed two lads heading their way. I quickly grabbed Colin and pulled him towards the girls saying you grab the shorter one. With that we just had the edge on them for speed, and luckily there was no need for confrontation, both girls at once said yes and that was the start of the rest of my life.

So, Colin, Joe, and myself, full of drink and riding on our success with the girls, clambered onto Colins scooter, we only had a short distance to go from the venue to our houses, Joe on the handlebars, Colin steering and me on the seat behind him. We negotiated the very steep hill that was at the beginning and the sharp corner at the bottom, as we went round it there was an old gentleman putting a hurricane lamp by the side of his car, in this period you had to have a parking light on the car or a lamp by the side of it. The look on his face at the site of three drunk lads on a scooter, there were no drink drive limits set at this time, forced him to leap out of the way knocking over the lamp, we zoomed off like three drunk hooligans. We went the longer way back home after that, usually on foot as I do not think Colin fancied a repetition of the experience.

Of course, this was the first meeting with Jacqueline and was at that time just another diversion in my life, all be it an exciting one. There was something about her that made me feel that I had known her all my life, of course that was impossible, I had just seen her somewhere before, there were a few other places with music in the area.

This time in my life and I guess every other person of my age, was fast moving, everything happened at breakneck speed and every young person was desperate to balance a career, with further education, travel, entertainment, love, sex, rock, and roll. What an exciting age in a person's life. It happens to every generation, but every generation is a unique one and, in most cases, vastly different to the preceding, and following generations yet to happen.

But every generation believes it is the best one and that makes for misunderstandings and conflicts between each existing and emerging generation. They call it the generation gap, ours was more of a chasm between us and our parents.

But getting back to the roaring sixties, seventies and up to the 2000`s. There I was falling in love with this fantastic young woman, a woman who I wanted to be with as much as possible and could share everything with her, apart from the total dark side of my young life, the very element that made me feel alone sometimes and doubting the reason for my very existence or even if I could ever be happy with life.

At this time, my father was still alive and being extra charming to my girlfriend Jackie, this caused further problems between him and myself, as because of his gambling problem I ended up having to pay for repairs on his van so that I could have transport to get to Jackie's house and go out evenings.

Problems that came purely because of his jealousy of my freedom and happiness. It was only after we were married that I told her some of the things that had happened with him, and she began to see his false identity crumble.

For us though everything was exciting, and we were making what would be new history, some good and some bad. I was still at the dockyard finishing my apprenticeship, but unfortunately, because of many distractions I lost the plot as they say and failed my end of year exams. Jackie was terribly upset and blamed our relationship for this incident. I assured her it was not the cause and that I would re-sit the examinations after another year of challenging work.

She stood by me and encouraged me to work and study, so that I could achieve my aims in life, and we could get married and have a happy life. With her support I did achieve all my goals and I have never forgot all her love and encouragement. I always wish that I could have told her everything about my early life, but that may never be, just what is in this story.

It hurts me to even think back to some of the things that happened. And now I still question if they were fact or fiction, or a bit of both. So, because of this wonderful woman I was able to get a full-time job as an electrician at the Dockyard.

Jackie was born in the same year as the NHS was founded by Aneurin Bevan, 1948. He was hoping for good health care for all, little did he know it was to be used to hold the people to ransom seventy-one years later, on the pretext that there was the beginning of a pandemic that would destroy a fantastic number of people and would require the rule of dictatorship to be applied to 'save the people'.

The main reason given to support a colossal set of violations of human rights, was, without complete control of the people, regardless of their human rights, the once great NHS would collapse. This was proven, to be the biggest load of bullshit ever to be used to control people, by so called democratic governments, in the UK.

Of course, forty to sixty percent of the people knew the real reason, this being the total mismanagement and mis control of funds over the years, by all political parties in government and NHS senior personnel. I use the percentage figure at the beginning of this paragraph, because that is the basic figure for a democratic society to be just that. In fact, control relies on the division of people by their conflicting opinions, to succeed.

Which is why you need at least two parties to vote for. In fact, it is the same pot of money, differing only in the way it`s distributed.

Of course, there have been many lessons that have not been learnt, because we are all concerned with our individual needs. and a lot of incidents are in the past like the second world war, where the total disregard of known ruthless dictators' and their actions, were allowed to continue.

Democracy becomes dictatorship in disguise.

Because of the support of my girlfriend Jacqueline, I had the incentive I needed to concentrate on a future, that I then wanted with all my heart. On the surface she was quiet and gentle, but she was like me in her spirit and had quite a temper when roused.

We continued at this time to have fun times and enjoyed all the music scenes going on, we had been through many changes in music styles, but at this time the music scene was still exciting. We were around when the Beatles decided to do a one-off concert on the roof of the apple building as a finally. One of my drawings depict this, I have enclosed it as this was to be one of the last, they would perform together.

John Lennon as I stated previously, was shot by a nobody called Mark Chapman, at 11Pm on 8th December 1980. There were things happening in the world that actually passed me by, now every movement anywhere in the world is on the news and every media outlet instantaneously.

While we were beginning our new lives, Idi Amin, was in the British army, he and his friends within the governments began plotting the assassination of Milton Obote who led Uganda to independence from the UK, maybe why we once again turned our heads and looked the other way.

Amins rise to power was with military and financial support from UK and Israel. He finally broke ties with UK and nationalised all British owned Businesses. He was supported with millions of pounds in value, by our old friend Russia.

Even Czechoslovakia and East Germany were involved in Amins State Research Bureau. He was slaughtering the people in his land Uganda, between 1971 and 1979 and the Bastard was allowed to live. It is purported that David Owen had proposed the assassination of Amin, maybe the one thing he was right about. But our, and other gutless governments, allowed him to live a life of luxury until he finally died in 2003.

We need to remind ourselves that the world during our young lives, was a violent and ever-changing environment, just as it is now, so nothing changes. If it feels like it might then it can be stifled by creating a worldwide disaster and dividing not only countries, but people within each country.

My children, now older didn't appreciate that there were many places we could not travel to in our younger days, without paperwork, and cash or goods for bribes of border forces, and many areas required visitors to be escorted whilst there.

Despite this the worst violence against people, was a long way from our shores, and it wasn't until a lot longer that the full horror of the situations were brought into reality by the media published.

Going back to the story of my life and on the lighter side of life. One of the funniest of these I will never forget, was in the early days of our marriage, in fact just a few weeks after our return to our newly bought house, by the way at a mortgage repayment rate of 10%.

Jackie decided she would cook us a chicken dinner with all the trimmings, she worked away in the kitchen and began laying the table whilst I sat in eager anticipation of the meal. I was never very domesticated; I suppose because my mother did all the domestic chores, and I did not even question that way of living. There were delicious smells coming from the kitchen and I sat at the table in eager anticipation of a royal banquet.

Suddenly Jackie came into the dining room carrying the baking tray with the chicken resting between the potatoes, she did not seem pleased, in fact she shouted, 'look at the chicken, I started to carve it and its not cooked properly.' I made the mistake of saying 'it looks OK to me.' Wrong move.

She said in disgust 'what do you know, I have slaved all morning over this dinner, no help from you.' With that she threw the tray and chicken at me, which I managed to dodge. Wrong move number two, I thought if I lightened the situation, she would see the funny side of it. She then ran at me, unfortunately her thinking that I thought it was funny, infuriated her even more, she grabbed at me, and I unfortunately found it even funnier, but as the laughing made her stronger and me weaker, I thought it best to make a dash to the toilet.

I gave her a small push and got to the toilet and

quickly bolted the door. With that Jackie hit against the door, two or three times and then I heard her go out of the front door and slam it shut. I was still laughing, but not for long, as the lock had bent slightly, and I could not move the bar across. I then needed to climb out of the window, get my tools, unscrew the lock, and straighten it, then refix it to the door. Just as I was finishing off the job, Jackie arrived back. We both burst out laughing and that was the first married tiff we had.

Although we had a few arguments, they were minor, and we resolved them without the use of food or flying objects. I was lucky that she supported me on all the decisions I made in my career, even though some of them were taken in the heat of the moment.

The house we had was close to the Dockyard and my trusty bicycle got me there with the odd repair of a puncture or two. So, the new me was going to put aside the past and look forward to the future. I was beginning to enjoy learning a skill and I was able to understand all the information I had to absorb to allow me to progress through the demands of married life and career development.

At this time, I had not had very many incidents or weird dreams although I still tried to move objects with my mind and only managed to get as far as the green surround, so maybe everything I had thought was in fact just fantasy. Then one night my sister Lynda came from her work to visit with us, and I offered to take her back to my parents' home in the car. It was a cold and foggy evening, so we set off and took the usual cut through which meant going down a winding steep hill that was quite narrow. We turned into it and the fog was worsening so I slowed up, as we reached the first bend in the road, without thinking I did an emergency stop and the car hit the curb and the engine cut out. As Lynda looked quizzically at me a car came speeding around the corner with no lights on, pursued by a police car. Lynda looked at me and said, 'how did you see that?' I simply replied 'I did not. 'I am quite sure she still remembers that incident, even after all these years. If I had not braked and stalled the car, we would have had a head on collision, at a speed of about ninety miles per hour and been in a three-car pileup.

I am not sure Jackie thought it was as dramatic as I did, and to be fair you had to be there to see the whole incident.

Getting back to the progression of my career, my skipper, as they were known in the dockyard, taught me everything I knew in the electrical field. He was an exceptional person and became my second father, the light side rather than the dark side. He was however the most accident-prone person I have ever known, as well as being the funniest without knowing it. Some of these incidents I just must share with you, there are so many situations that I could fill this whole book with them but for now just a few tasters.

Chapter 20

Skipper Jack

His name was Jack, I am sure that song, back in my youth, with the words 'my name is Jack and I lived in the back of the Gretta Garbo home, for wayward boys' and girls' was about him.

He began his life as an orphan, living at a Doctor Barnardo's home with his brother, after leaving there, he met his wife Wyn, a servant at a manor house, who I must admire as the most tolerant of people, second only to my own wife.

His mode of transport was a moped, this had a mind of its own and decided when it would start and when it would not, usually at home time it would decide to refuse to start up just to bring Jack to a state of despair.

I used to have a pushbike and all bikes had to be pushed up to and out of the gate. This was a requirement for everyone possessing a motorbike and of course moped.

Because of its refusal to conform with Jacks instructions, he used to switch off the engine at the very last second which ment on this day I was walking beside him talking, he had been late getting back to the workshop so had decided to keep his overalls on. He began his ritual of turning off the engine and then as we passed through the gate, he gave a large push, he then engaged the gear just as he passed through, this ment that the engine started every time, he then jumped on and was away heading for home.

this time unfortunately, being distracted by talking to me, he had not noticed that the bottoms of his oversized overalls were close to the exposed flywheel and now as the obedient moped started up, the bottom of the overalls wound into the flywheel which gave a sudden pull on his leg. This in turn unbalanced him resulting in him hopping at breakneck speed behind the moped made worse by the fact that the motion caused him to grip the throttle pulling it towards him, so increasing the speed of the moped.

The scene was like something out of the old silent movies, everyone dispersing in all directions trying to avoid this crazy moped pursued by an old hopping man shouting expletives. Eventually he came to a halt with my help, having discarded my bicycle so further adding to the total chaos at the exit from the dockyard. Apart from torn overalls cuts and bruises he was ok.

This was the beginning of a trilogy of events which resulted in a broken wrist and two broken collar bones all within weeks of each other. Every incident went from a disaster to a comic interlude, simply by the reaction of Jack, why couldn't he have been my father? I guess then I would not be me, I do not know if that would have been good or bad.

The second incident began with a telephone call from Jack's wife Wyn, telling me that jack was in hospital with a broken wrist and could I pick him up in my car and put the moped in the back. Ominous I thought, but Wyn would only say 'You have to ask him what happened yourself I will never be able to get to the end of the story.' I agreed to pick him up, especially now I was intrigued to know what had happened.

I arrived at the hospital and there was Jack waiting around the back of the entrance area with his moped, the moped being a little bent and worse for wear, Jacks hand and wrist in plaster and strapped in a sling around his neck. My first reaction was to ask, 'what the hell happened this time.' Thinking of course the same thing must have happened again with the exposed fly wheel and trouser incident.

Once in the car he began with 'you won't believe it I was coming over Rochester bridge and being it was very windy, taking extra care, up in front were two young women one pushing a pram, there was a sudden gust of wind.' You can imagine I at once thought he was going to say it blew him into the two women and the pram. He continued 'The girl on the outside was wearing a short dress and it blew up revealing that she had a bare arse, well the guy driving the car just passing me, must have had a full view like me and with the shock of it he ran into me and knocked me off the moped, mind you she did have a nice arse.' Well, this I thought had to be the most bizarre way to get a broken bone ever. But no, the second call from Wyn, was the tops, in my view.

This was about two months on from the last incident at the bridge, again triggered by a telephone call from Wyn, this time it was that Jack was in hospital with two broken collar bones, this time not caused by the moped but his bicycle. Again, Wyn wanted to leave the explanation to Jack as she found it difficult to explain the first few sentences of the incident without laughing. Trying to predict the conclusion to the explanation, I could not even dream what would make the breaking of both collar bones, even the slightest bit funny, let alone hilarious.

I arrived at the hospital and sure enough after finding the ward, there he was, propped up in the bed looking sorry for himself. As soon as I sat down, even before I asked how he was, I asked how it could have been possible to break both collar bones falling off a bicycle? Get prepared with a box of tissues here goes bad language included, this was his explanation. In his own words.

'It began with Irene (youngest unmarried daughter), telling me she was pregnant and adding that she didn`t know how it had happened. I was so upset I decided to go up the club for a few pints to drown my sorrows, so I went on the bicycle to avoid any problems with the police if I got stopped on the moped. The problem started when I had more than I intended and felt a bit worse for wear. I did not want to bother you, so I decided to ride the bike back as its all downhill.'

Just to give the picture from the club down to the bottom of the hill is a narrow twisting road with trees either side spaced at quite wide intervals from each other, an ideal coast down on a bicycle, no kerbs to worry about just a grass verge either side.

'I was enjoying the fresh air and getting up quite a nice speed, on one of the bends a car was coming up the hill at quite a speed and I moved over, due to my judgment being a little off, due to the drink. I hit the grass verge and mounted the verge going head long into a tree, this tree had a Y shape trunk, and my head went through the Y shape smashing both my collar bones, so here I am. But do you know the worst thing.?' Intrigued by the story I answered 'No.' 'The copper who turned up with the ambulance said to me,' 'You must be the luckiest man alive, if you had been slightly to the left of the tree, your head would have smashed into the bough, and you could have died or sustained brain damage'. 'I just stared at him and replied, what are you talking about, Lucky?

There's not another fucking tree around for two hundred yards and I have two broken collar bones and you call that luck?'

After laughing uncontrollably for some considerable time, I got back to Jacks first revelation and asked about his reaction to Irene's announcement that she was pregnant and did not know how it had happened, totally missing the point, he replied, 'I told her I would know if someone shoved a rod up my arse.' Again, I had a fit of laughter, I do not think he had any Idea of the misinterpretation of her meaning.

Jack played an exceptionally large part in my life and without the two people, who coincidentally or maybe by design had the same name by gender Jack and Jackie. If not for both their influences on my progression through life, I am sure the outcome would have been significantly different. They managed to calm my anger, even though I caused them some anger, not being the most straight forward of people to deal with. Do not worry it does not get boring from here onwards, well not for me anyway, you may disagree.

Back to Jack, in the time when he was still my skipper, I guess apart from when he decided to run along the joists in the Admiralty house, resulting in him falling through the ceiling and landing on a chandelier, which had been previously, removed from its place for cleaning. This was not his funniest incident, just the result of him being clever by trying to show off, mocking my cautious movements when I was just a young lad and should be twice as athletic as him. Luckily, for me. I was twice as clever.

We were still in the administration block conducting repairs and had positioned our table for our break time and lunch, in the corridor. This ment that the people in the office, all female, had to pass by us to get to the exit door.

This time we were playing cards and I was winning all the hands, as two of the women passed our table, I had yet again trumped Jacks card, engrossed in the game, he stood up shouting 'fuck it.' at the very moment the girls passed by, they giggled but Jack was mortified. All he kept on saying was, 'I will have to apologise when they come back, let me know the moment you see them.' I told him not to worry, they had heard it all the time, women swear as well as men, sometimes worse. But he was not convinced by me.

Suddenly, the two women came through the large swing doors entering the corridor. Jack at once stood up and as they got to us, he said, and I quote. 'Excuse me, I am very sorry that I said that bad swear word in front of you two lovely ladies, I just didn't see you please forgive me, I felt a right c—t.' There was complete silence and even Jack was lost for words. The youngest woman of the two saved the day for Jack, she winked at him and said, whilst walking away. 'I know you didn't mean to say that you can't help being a silly old prick.' I was in hysterics and intermittently bursting into laughter for the rest of the day.

After Jack had finally retired and I had progressed to a manager in the dockyard and put on a section dealing with the site services with the grand status of working in the nuclear section.

Part of my responsibilities were the normal site services within the nuclear site, these were not bound in secrecy, especially the control of sewage leaving site after a good night by the naval personnel staying in the on-site accommodation.

Chapter 21

Where did the lump go?

So here is one tale that I cannot let pass by. Because of the size of the area, there were two injection pits, 'deep pits holding high pressure pumps designed to pump the sewerage out to the main sewerage line, which ended up at the treatment works. I had a call that the pumps in one of the pits had stopped working. Normally a simple job of reversing the pump motors to unblock the system. Two of us arrived to find that the pit was indeed beginning to fill up, so after drawing straws to see which one of us would have to go down in the pit and reverse the pump connections,

I descended the ladder to conduct the operation. The smell was horrific almost pure methane. I conducted the simple operation and switched back on the pumps but no joy. This was now a big problem as we had not brought a transfer pump with us, and the pit was filling quickly.

Luckily for us an extremely helpful naval officer was at hand, the very person that had reported the problem to our section. 'Don't worry old chaps' he said and ordered his crew members to fetch a pump, off they went at top speed and returned with a large and incredibly old diesel pump, under his orders they pushed the hose on the suction side of the pump down the rapidly filling injection pit and pushed the delivery hose down the spare pit tying it to the top of the steps, to ensure it was held firm at the end. I could not believe the state of the delivery hose it looked like it had come off HMS victory. I told him it was not a promising idea to use the hose especially as it was tied at the end. He told me plainly that he knew far more than a dockyard worker and he would take charge of the operation.

At this point I told the youth with me to come with me behind the pump pit protection wall and heard the officer shout out, 'start her up on my command,' there was a very brief interlude and then the command came. The pump roared into action and in a matter of seconds there was a loud sound and great activity. I looked around the corner of the wall and there was chaos, the large hose was flapping around uncontrollably, three sailors were trying to hold the pump and switch it off, which they did. There against the opposite wall, was the officer pinned against it covered in excrement, the sailors rushed to him and peeled him from the wall leaving the outline of his body on the wall. I called the dockyard surgery to get an ambulance, as I did not know exactly how much he had inhaled.

Amazingly nobody had time to take in the situation until he left to go to the local hospital. A quick-thinking sailor had got a new hose and we fitted it to the pump, dropped it into the pit and pumped the sewerage from one pit to the other, with only a small amount of extra spillage.

It was not until we had everything under control, that we looked up to see on the very top of a crane a single large lump of manure stuck to the jib. We had a bet on how long it would take to fall, as the crane was not in use very often, it disappeared after two days but we never knew what had happened to it, its destination was a mystery, that to this day intrigues me. Where did the lump go??? We never did discover the answer to that question. There were however other incidents that I did know the answers to, one was the day the heating in the guard's office went off due to an unknown electrical fault that took four hours to trace. The cause was found to be a particular guard who thought he had been given the position as chief gestapo of the nuclear site security and decided to evaluate his authority over me, wrong move.

It was a hectic morning and there were a lot of minor faults caused by a night of thunderstorms, because the equipment was susceptible to ground faults, the safety trips were sensitive to prevent any safety problems and alarm out. This ment there were few real safety problems but a lot of need to manually reset systems. This ment that I had to go out to every alarm and check the system and reset if everything checked out ok. Every time I entered the site, I had to hand over my pass to the security and every exit I had to collect the pass.

After passing through about six times on this morning that was freezing cold, I was waiting to collect my pass to get out. The window was closed to keep in the warm air in the security hut and the two guards were chatting together, I waited for at least five minutes and there was no movement from them, so I knocked on the window, no response other than a quick glance towards me. I then kept knocking on the window until Mr gestapo opened the panel and started to lecture me about how many times I had been through the gate and how every time he opened the window, they lost heat in the room. I was incredibly pleased with myself and replied that I was having to reset systems as they alarmed out and I was freezing as well, he just grunted and threw my pass at me. Again, I kept complete control of my temper and took the pass. I waited for ten minutes in one of the substations where it was nice, warm, and happened to hold the fuse board with the electrical switch system for the guard house, so I switched it off and returned to my office. Within five minutes I had a call from, non-other than Mr gestapo, complaining that the lights and power including the heating was off. I told him I would get there as soon as possible. One hour later I had a call from head of security asking what was happening as there was no heating and lighting in the nuclear security hut. I told him I was waiting on a new breaker to fit. I then took a gentle stroll to the substation and switched on the breaker, I then returned to the security hut, tapped on the window Mr G opened it, I asked him if he was warm now and held his look as I said in my mind arsehole, do you know I think he read my mind he looked down to the ground. After that I never had my pass thrown at me again. I was learning at last.

Finally, I had discovered. This was where the lump of manure was all along.

It had taken human form and dressed up in a uniform.

Chapter 22

Peace at last

During this period of my life, I was concentrating on my new family and work responsibilities and had little time to dedicate to the home life I had left behind, but of course I was still close to my mother, sisters, and little brother, who appeared eleven years after me.

My Father went into hospital for an operation as he had been suffering with chest pains, we had notification that he was to be released from hospital and sent home. Could we find transportation as there was a shortage of ambulances. Sounds familiar? I took my mother to the hospital to collect him. But before we went into the waiting room to get him, we spoke to his consultant.

He explained that my father had lung cancer, but they had not been able to remove it, so he would not survive past about six months.

He did not want clarification of his condition, typical of his usual attitude to deny everything if he had any thought that it might not be what he wanted to hear. So, he left mother to bear the news, and decide whether to tell him.

I drove him home in silence, my mother was issued a wheelchair by the hospital, and he could still get up and walk, and at first even get up to the toilet. I visited my mother to support her, and this visit he decided to ask me what was wrong with him, as he felt sick all the time. I just answered him truthfully, 'you have terminal cancer.' He looked at me in a pathetic sort of way and said, 'does that mean I am going to die?' I thought of a lot of responses, but decided a simple yes was all it needed. 'When, he asked?' I just replied 'soon.' With that I turned and walked out of the house. A few weeks later my mother rang and asked if I would visit as he had been asking to see me. By now he was in a bed in the lounge, where he could watch the tv set in the corner with the understairs cupboard behind it. I must admit I was surprised how he had deteriorated in the few weeks since I had left him. He called me over to him and his first words to me were, 'help me they are in the cupboard, and they watch me all the time'.

I asked him what he was talking about, he replied 'the customs officers, they are in the cupboard behind the TV, they are coming after us. That is when I realised what he was on about. The cupboard was where he stored the boxes of groceries that he had forced me to make up at the shop all those years ago.

Not one word of remorse, in fact his exact words were coming after us, not him, I was beginning to think he believed I was a willing party to his antics. He then looked at me, putting on the most pathetic face you could imagine and said, in the most contrived pathetic voice,' please forgive me for everything, l just wanted you to be special, let me die in peace, say you will forgive me.'

I could only have ever given the reply I gave him, not out of pure malice as you may think, but to forgive someone on their deathbed had to mean something real and not just be cheap words that ment nothing, just like the ones he had just decided to share with me, to what end?

I could not then and will never forgive him.

I could see the tears in his eyes form and watched them run down his cheeks. Even then he could not say the words that may have moved me, the words that I had always wanted to believe. I love you.

I turned and walked out of the room.

My mother was in the kitchen, and we exchanged looks, she just said. 'I understand but you may change your mind in the morning, he needs you to forgive him before he can pass away,' she never did and never will know why that could have never been possible from then on.

She was deeply religious in fact an elder of the church. I could never believe that way. I tried religion and found its inescapable fundamental flaw, PEOPLE.

I just said the first thing that came into my mind to try to give her some comfort. 'Don`t worry he doesn't need me to forgive him, he will die today and that will be his release from me. And most of all his lies that we have all had to suffer.'

It took me about 30 minutes to get home, as I entered the house the telephone rang and my mother just said, 'How did you know? he died 10 minutes after you left, you knew didn't you'. As I put the telephone down a single tear formed in my right eye and ran down on to my cheek. I wiped it off in disgust, it was not for him but self-pity for me, I could never know the love of a father.

It is strange but from that day I never really thought about him, he just became a person I once knew and until I began this story, I did not consider the consequences of re-living the emotions a parent has on a child's life and a child on a parent. I just wished I could have asked him something I never even thought to ask in all those years, why?

My new priority was to look after my wife and to take control of my life and build a future for us and our children.

So going forward in the dockyard I decided, I would go for promotion this meant carrying on with my exams and getting as far as I could with my higher national certificate in electrical engineering, then I could apply for a job in the office as an estimating engineer, which I did. At first it was different, and I had a good section to look after, which involved travel to London locations looking after the work projects in the underground tunnels. But this was not a very well-paid job and to make ends meet I worked as a window cleaner with another guy in the office at the weekends. I even borrowed my fathers-in-law`s ladder, this extra cash meant we could have holidays with the children.

This was not really what I wanted, but myself and a young guy on the mechanical engineering side, got to produce a system of estimation of the time and the operations required, to safely complete a nuclear submarine refit, this was a remarkably interesting project, and we produced a programme that was used on the refits of a nuclear submarine within Chatham dockyard.

Now full of optimism, I decided it was time to try to go a little higher in status and become what was known as an inspector, to do this you had to take an interview, as well as have the written qualifications. I worked nights and went off to college, not sleeping for two nights a week to ensure I had those qualifications. After I got the certificates I applied for the position, certain that I would get it. I usually got the choice to take everything I went after; I never had any doubts about my ability. I applied and got an interview with the head of the section, in our case ahead of yard services. Then on his recommendation you could be given the opportunity to take promotion when an opening came along.

Well unfortunately my interview was a complete disaster, the main reason being that the head of the department did not know who I was, this was quite clear as only three days before, he congratulated myself and the mechanical engineer, for producing the nuclear refit programme and praised our dedication to the success of the yard services division.

I could not really believe this was the extent of the civil service senior personnel. Of course, time has proven that all government departments through time, and right up to the present consist of insincere nobodies, with little knowledge or understanding of the requirements of their skills and dedication to be effective in their roles.

Unfortunately, I decided at that time to get up from the table and tell him exactly what he could do with his job and where he could stick it, going home and telling Jacqueline began to make me regret my rash decision but it clearly did not her, she said something like, 'well if the guy doesn't know you after he actually praised you in front of everybody three days before, then yes perhaps you should leave'. So again, she was on my side, and much later she walked away from similar situations, with the clear understanding that I would back her in any decision on her working life.

I then decided to go to a local job seekers/agency, and after a brief time I had an interview at a local business establishment as a works engineer. During the lead up to this we had moved home, as we now had two children so needed a three-bedroom house, this one was also semi-detached with a substantial size garden. In the garden I had made a little playhouse for the children, they called it Matt Beck cottage.

It was in our next house that I experienced yet another sign to let me know, whatever the experience was, it remained with me wherever I went. Our new house had a top room set into the loft space, we used this as a games room, the stairs were at the end of the landing opposite the bathroom. During this period of time my grandmother fell ill and passed away.

We were dressing to go up to see my mother and go through my grandmothers' belongings. I caught sight of my daughter going up to the loft room in a white lace dress. I had not seen it before, so I called out to her to let me have a look at her new dress.

At this point I froze and felt extreme coldness. She turned, but I realised it was not my daughter. The figure looked directly at me and said clearly in a normal voice. 'Don't worry Keith I am with Harry now; we are just leaving together now.' With that she continued up the stairs. I froze for a few seconds, then I rushed along the landing and went up to the loft room. It was empty, just freezing cold. I ran down the stairs and into the kitchen, where everyone was sitting waiting for me. Jackie staired at me and asked if I was ill, because I was as white as a sheet. She then joked saying 'have you seen a ghost?' I just simply replied 'I think I did.' I explained to her my experience, nothing I ever told her really surprised her.

During that day, my mother was going through my grandmothers' possessions, with me. I opened a letter from my grandmother to my grandfather and in it was a picture of the girl I saw at the stairs to the loft room. It was her in the same white dress. I could not bear to tell her I had seen this same person at the foot of the stairs in my house that same morning.

All I could think of doing was to ask my mother if I had ever seen the letter before. Her reply was No She had never seen it either. It was in with a bunch of letters, returned from the hospital when my grandfather died and locked in my grandmother's bedside drawer.

Jackie looked at me and all I could do was walk away and do something in the garden, to look like I was tidying up.

We did discuss the situation when we got back home, and the Children were in bed. But as in most cases it was just an indefinable happening, sometime somewhere I had seen the letter and photograph.

Getting back to the mundane things in life from the supernatural to the chores of finding a new job.

I had a couple of interviews one was as a lighting design engineering company in Croydon, and had an offer of employment, but eventually I could not get the right money to allow me to move to London, so I had to look again.

The second interview was a total disaster, I walked out halfway through the interview, I knew I could never collaborate with the guy that would have been my boss. Jackie again supported me on both these decisions.

I then had the third interview, Jackie saw this in the local paper and pointed it out to me, they had finished the interviews but were not happy with the candidates and if I could come straight away, they would interview me. I took the interview and was offered the job at the interview; I accepted the offer, and this was the start of my next adventure into the private workforce as opposed to the civil service, all due to the continuing support of Jackie a true partner in everything.

Chapter 23

Doc the knife

Strangely at this late stage of my younger life, I was to discover that in fact not only tolerance to ordinary pain was no longer the same as I remembered in my years before my dream of being knifed by the red eyed shadow. I was also to discover that anaesthetics including local anaesthetics did not work in the normal way on me.

Still the most memorable introduction to this realisation came when Jackie and I decided that we had the family we were happy with, three children, and I would have a vasectomy to ensure we would not have any more, a good sign that even then we were sure we would always be together.

So off I went for this simple operation, in, quick snip and back home within a couple of hours, all under local anaesthetic. This was the first operation I had experienced, apart from having a tooth out under gas, yes gas fed through a gas mask. I was on this occasion, injected with the local anaesthetic and taken into the operation room for the simple snip.

The operation began, at first, I just felt a slight tickle, is the best way to explain it. Then very shortly after I felt an excruciating pain which made me cry out. Everyone froze and the surgeon asked did you feel that, to which I replied as calmly as I could, 'yes it felt like you were pulling something out of my body' he replied quite calmly. 'I was tying off your tube, we will have to inject some more anaesthetic, but I will have to finish this first.' Do not ask me why but I just told him to continue. He said, 'I have only just started, so I will do a second injection in a few seconds, I will give you the maximum.' He muttered something about unbelievable, there is nothing on his notes. With this I felt the second injection being administered, I had a feeling of a coldness coming over me, just like the feeling in my bedroom.

He waited for about five minutes, although it felt like a lifetime. The young nurse at the operation said to me 'you will be alright now; you have enough anaesthetic inside of you to knock out an elephant.' Everyone took their positions and resumed the operation. I can remember the reaction clearly, forty years later. I felt no actual acute pain but calmly said 'I can feel you cutting me now.' This time the doctor seemed unsure of what to do, I said 'just get on with it.' He told the nurse to deal with me and keep talking to me, she attached a blood pressure machine to me and although I could not see it, she watched it intently whilst asking me all about what I did, the sports I liked and other unrelated topics, clearly to divert my attention from the procedures around my lower end. The doctor to his credit finished the procedure and I was rushed to the treatment room where a bed had been placed circled with a curtain. Fully awake I asked what was happening,

I was told that my blood pressure had reached an elevated level and I could not be discharged until it had reached an acceptable level. I was never told how high it reached and never was interested. However, the young nurse, whilst trying to distract me during the operation, had asked if the reason for the operation had been worth the pain. I had replied I hope so fun without worry. She replied with, I was now safe, in fact I was certainly not going to be able to think about sex for a long time hinting that the amount of local anaesthetic would prevent me from 'getting an erection for a long time.'

She took my blood pressure and said I will just check everything is OK below and with a smile rolled up the blankets and lifted the gown. With that her eyes widened, she gasped a little and then turned and ran out of the door. I was shocked and assumed she had gone out to get the surgeon because something had burst maybe. But she returned, not with the surgeon but with the other nurse in the operation and a ward sister, who happened to be my aunt. 'Look, look' she said 'unbelievable.' Everyone stared in amazement, I very slowly looked down and there in the centre of a black mass of bruises was the largest erection I had ever experienced and will ever experience. I don't know what I expected but certainly not that. My aunt was incredibly good and did not mention it again.

Since this experience I discovered that local anaesthetics had extraordinarily insignificant effect on me, in fact I had a few problems with doctors not believing the incident was due to my resistance rather than not enough anaesthetic administered. The advantage is that I am quite resistant to pain, immensely helpful on several occasions during my life.

Anyway, let us travel back in time to the good old days, we can do that in this story because I am not sure, sometimes if the future is now, and the past was the future.

This job was ideal for me; it was the type of business where it depended on you being good enough to stick to your views and strong enough to hold your own, against what was a predominant number of women workers.

My method of management was learnt on the job, there is now a trend towards set training of how to be a manager, in fact a lot of money is made on providing courses to train managers, often run by failed managers, not because they do not know the theory behind being a good manager of people, but my opinion, it is a skill that does not follow a blueprint, it is just either built in you or not. The main thing is to be decisive, consistent, fair, and always make sure you know all your workers and never assume about a person. To this day I do not know why but I had this uncanny way of being able to read their moods and hidden reactions to instructions or incidents relating to my interactions with them.

Along with this came a useful biproduct in seeming to be able to get people to believe in what I did, what I was doing and what I was saying, which is a significant help as far as management is concerned.

There were quite a few incidents I experienced at this workplace and eventually all the things I learned helped me very much as I progressed.

One I will always remember, which was the most nerve racking of my whole career involved a group of unruly middle aged women, who decided to capitalise on the then up and coming strength of the unions and their shop stewards, often voted in to the position because of their associates or because no one else wanted to be in the position, which gave them the ability to get a gang of discontented people fired up enough, to face, very often a single manager.

This group of women were headed up by the shop steward, a large scary woman with zero respect for management, or indeed anyone not having the same thoughts as her. Disaster was bound to come my way, as the personnel manager, known today as 'the head of human resources, 'more bullshit, was not able to confront this type of individual. So, I was asked if I could deal with an incident, which was happening in the ladies' cloak room between this woman and her group of friends and a couple of the women workers.

The explanation of the incident relayed to me, was that this small group of women were sitting amongst people's coats and eating food, whilst wiping their mouths on peoples' coats. So off I went into the lady's cloakroom, where could at once hear raised voices, using, what could only be described, as the worst foul language. Luckily, the ringleader was the shop steward, so I asked in a loud voice. 'Is this an official trade union meeting, or one which has happened without notifying the personnel department?'

The shop steward staired at me and shouted, 'Fuck off this has nothing to do with you.' I just staired at her and said in a normal voice level. 'As everything that happens, in every area that my department has to maintain, it has everything to do with me, so I suggest you all leave this area and either go back to your place of work, or out into the yard.' One of her cronies replied, 'piss off or we will all throw you out into the yard.' Without moving my eyes from the shop steward, I replied 'I think something has just made a statement, which will cause those thinking it's that simple, to end up either in hospital, sacked or both. Your choice.'

There was complete silence, where our eyes held each other's gaze, I tried to give a blank expression, which obviously gave no sign of any emotion I had. She then looked away and said to her cronies, 'come on let's get away from this prick.' I at once replied, 'No you two stay, I do not know your names, (which was, of course false, and they knew it), so for now I'll call you dumb and dumber. Obviously, this had never happened before because neither knew what to do or say so everyone else headed for the door, much simpler than to question the rights or wrongs of the situation, leaving the two of them totally isolated with no one to feed off. The classic DIVIDE AND CONQUER.

Much later in this story, the tact used by our government and the democratic governments of the so-called free world, to destroy democracy and rule with fear. Sounds dramatic but remember this incident.

Just out of interest the two women were issued with a written warning and the cloakrooms locked during the work period, they could still sneak a quick cigarette in the toilets, but nobody's clothes were contaminated by smoke and food, so everyone above the level of a slob benefited and I became an acceptable member of the senior management, by the workforce.

I learnt a lot about management at this location and carried it forward onto my next promotion, which meant that I ended up in the head office of the same Company, at a London location known as Brimsdown, where I was eventually employed, as works engineering manager. So continues the story of my progression through the workplaces.

This place in my development was undoubtedly the biggest and most influential, teaching me about the complete range of skills needed to take a person, what I call 'to their level of incompetence.'

The management team here were very much together and our equivalent of a managing director level was a skilful man manager and kept a smooth-running operation, unfortunately the product produced at the factory was at the end of its life, namely flashcubes for cameras. This was the beginning of built-in flashes and like every technological advance, it comes with consequences.

Once again, my luck was being at the right place at the right time and because of this I was offered, a move to the large site in north London housing three different Companies. The interesting thing was, not only was I to be the deputy works Engineer, but I was also given the task of looking after the buildings we were to evacuate, the existing local factory that had been closed for over a year, and an operational factory in south London. This ment that I did not have to re-locate to north London and could organise my travel schedule.

The biggest problem was that I was moving into what was known as a corporate position and my genuine experience at this level being only twenty-six was, limited. As it worked out, this was my biggest asset, things had progressed so quickly that I did not have any idea of the size of job or the final responsibilities and direction my career was going, so I did not have time to contemplate how I would tackle incidents that would present themselves. The main thing is to quickly understand the level of interaction possible, between the person you are interacting with.

To gauge their responses, start off putting them out of their comfort zone not straight into the issue requiring the resolution, they would have practiced their excuse repeatedly.

So off I went on my first day at the new position, first mistake I had not accounted for the level of traffic going from Kent up to North London via the Blackwall tunnel. So, I left at seven o`clock in the morning, as I was meeting my new boss at 11 o`clock, plenty of time. After two and a half hours I was in a massive traffic jam in the centre of the Blackwall tunnel, bursting for a pee. I knew my sister-in-Law lived close by, so at the point of losing control of my bladder, I arrived outside her flat. I dived out of the car and rang her doorbell, standing on her doorstep wiggling uncontrollably. The door opened, I said' hi must use your loo.' pushed past her and dived up her stairs and into the toilet. She has never let me forget that incident, mainly because I came out of the toilet completely relieved, kissed her on the cheek and said, 'can't stay I need to get to

Brimsdown for a meeting.' With that I got in the car and drove off.

I had a reasonable drive for the remaining part of the journey, and eventually arrived at the site, I then discovered the size and responsibility of my position. Firstly, my boss the works Engineer was off sick with a heart murmur, which meant I had to take over as his position until he returned. I had two secretaries, head of electrical engineering, head of Mechanical engineering, two boilermen responsible for the total site heating, head of buildings building repairs on all factories and site security. The total workforce amounting to fifty-eight people which included no less than four union shop stewards. To top it all the unions had called for industrial action, due to a very unpopular re-organisation of the site resulting in pending redundances. This certainly was not the best day of my life, even though my wages had increased by a third, my stress levels had increased by three-fold.

Chapter 24

Meet the troupes

I decided that I would meet with my new boss directly after lunch, giving me time to organise a meeting with everyone together in our massive workshop, and get it over in one foul swoop, then I would hopefully know how things stood with this industrial relations problem, which I knew nothing of, until I arrived on my first day.

I could hear them all arriving in the workshop as my office was directly over the corner of the second floor. I took a deep breath and told Norma and Margaret to lead on and I would follow her down to the meeting.

I entered the room where I faced a mass of people, older than me by a number of years, and all of them disgruntled, it did not begin very well, as the front five people were the union shop stewards, it happened a great percentage of them worked for my departments. I introduced myself as the new deputy works engineer, one of the shop stewards asked me, with a hint of sarcasm, well are you in charge because George is out sick? As if that ment anything to me, and the girls cannot help you because we are pulling them out on strike tomorrow, so you will not be able to fill in the time sheets.

I must confess I had obviously made a mistake by not meeting my new boss first, I had no idea that I was heading up the whole operation without any support. Looking full of confidence, I said the first thing that came into my head. 'Ok that means there will be no overtime just flat rate payments, until we can fill in the time sheets.' It looked like none of the shop stewards had considered the consequences of the statement of action. One of course had an immediate answer to banter with me. 'Then the production department won't be able to work the second shift' This was becoming fun, I replied 'well luckily, I am not in charge of production, so I guess there will not be a second shift, and they will be on flat money without a production bonus, I assume you have discussed this with everyone?' You could have heard a pin drop, there was absolute silence. A few exchanged glances making it obvious that the statement had indeed, not been discussed with the remaining shop stewards of the various factory workers.

I then, feeling uncomfortable despite my bravado, finished by saying, 'well it was good to meet you all, if any of you want to discuss anything with me, I will be upstairs.' with that I turned around and went up the stairs to my office. I could hear a lot of loud voices in argument with each other and the odd, 'he's just a boy, he won't last five minutes.'

My first baptism by fire and it was not to be my last by a long way. Now I was to learn everything I had ever wanted to, not just a trade, but a whole understanding of the workings of the human being at all levels, along with skills in areas I had never dreamed of. But in the end, it was only ever about knowing the levels of understanding and needs of the people you are dealing with and being able to communicate at each level without being patronising or dismissive of their feelings.

Now I had to do the same with the so-called senior management personnel, my colleagues.

So, who is first? My direct boss the works engineer George, was off sick. He was promoted around six months before I arrived, this was after, the works Engineer, a guy called Earnie (yes ironically the same name as my father). Left to run his own business.

The senior person, who was second in command at the site was a guy who again ironically, had the same name as me Keith. I arranged to see him straight after the meeting with my workforce. Up to now I had no idea of what my job entailed, other than it was heading up the site engineering trades. So now I was to discover the full extent of the job I had eagerly accepted, which had already taken me to levels of responsibilities far more than any of my experiences up to now.

I was met, by Keith's secretary, who led me into his office, he stood up and shook my hand, his first words being. 'Well Keith, I have been talking to George and he has asked me, that due to his heart attack, is it possible that you would officially accept the position of Works engineer and George take your place as deputy works engineer, when he returns to work? Mr King has agreed to the proposal.'

I was absolutely dumfounded, I just stared at first, not actually totally understanding the words I was hearing. I do not think I had processed any of the words, but my mouth formed the answer, 'OK as long as I am paid at the works engineer's rate?' His reply without any hesitation was 'Of course, you will clarify that with Mr King tomorrow.' King being the managing director of the complete site, God himself.

First, though I had to have an interview with the site personnel manager, known now by the grand title, Human resources director. I must confess that I was confused, an interview to see if I was going to get the job? Hardly, I had just had promotion, before beginning the position first offered, and the personnel manager, unbeknown to him, was now at an equal position as me.

Anyway, I did not have a problem meeting the guy and letting him ask me a few questions to show that the site procedures had been adhered to. So we began, first the formal introductions, his name was Gerry, niceties over he began my interview, we got to the formal appraisal of my suitability in controlling a workforce of over fifty people. I thought how do I know; I have never had more than ten people working under my supervision. I was about to answer with the words in my head when he continued with. 'What if you gave someone a direct instruction and he refused to do as instructed by you.' This was I thought a simple one, thoughts of the woman in the cloakroom, I replied with the real live scenario of the cloakroom drama. Even before I had completed my explanation Gerry butted in, 'Ah but what if it was a Man and he threatened you with violence' he said. I just staired at him and said, 'would you'? Luckily, I think my look was enough to give him a feeling that he did not want to pursue the line of questioning, but by now I was losing my patients, so I finished with 'in any case I have a second in command, three foremen a chargehand and six security guards, how big is this bastard going to be, because I didn't see anyone at my meeting that frightening'. We shook hands, confirming I was now Works Engineer.

I was now to meet the King, as he was referred to by his subjects. This meeting was to plan for a complete re-organisation and reduction of the site. Reducing the number of individual companies and move some of those operations to different locations within the group, some being as far away as the Northeast of England.

The intensity of this encounter gave me the solid grounding and self-confidence to take me to places and give me skills I had never dreamed were possible for me to ever master, and further build on. Should I ever consider that the influences were coming from somewhere other than sheer luck, or being at the right place at the right time? I should, even now I can never get that dark figure from the past completely out of my dreams, or Donavan himself.

I knocked on the Kings door and was invited in, he did not rise from his chair, just pointed to the chair in front of his desk and I was told to sit down. He pointed out that there was a plan table at the far end of the room, covered with site plans, the three walls surrounding the table were full of papers, schedules, and more site plans with brightly coloured highlights.

I was told that he was a chain smoker and at that time there was no considerations made for people, males or females who hated breathing in second hand nicotine.

He highlighted the thinking behind the plans for the scheduled re-configuring of the site operations. He then got up from his desk and began walking towards the end of the room holding the plans, a lighted cigarette between two fingers of his right hand, the ones discoloured to a dark yellow from knuckle to the fingertips. As we began discussing the positions of the various machines, he suddenly stopped, turned, and began walking back to his desk, where he, on arrival flicked the ash of his cigarette into his ashtray, turned around and walked back to the plans at the other end of the room with me in tow.

After the fourth trip I knew I had to do something about the situation, or we would never last the day out. Even though I did not smoke other than the odd cigarette to be sociable, I told him that I had left my cigarettes in my office, so could I have one of his to tide me over, to my surprise he at once offered me one and lit it for me. We then went ahead to walk from one end of the room to the other to deposit ash into the ash tray. Perfect as he lit up his next cigarette, I tactfully suggested that it would be more time saving if we transported the ashtray to the plans on the wall and back to the desk at the end of our discussions in that area of the room.

I will never know whether it was a test to see my tolerance level, or to see if I could become his yes man, or some other bizarre reason but he moved the ashtray and repositioned it at the end of our meeting. He was, later to realise that I was the only one that showed him any respect at all, while his old cronies deserted him completely.

As I left Kings office, Keith Room invited me back to his office, intrigued to know what was happening, as he could see us walking to and frow from his window. I relayed the situation to him, which gave him a good laugh and me a little bit more credibility.

Later I discovered by chance that the other site directors, all much older than me, hated the fact that I could manage the King, and they weren't even happy that he allowed me to wear a leather Jacket (given to me by my mother-in-law), to the board meetings. Did they tell me this? No, I happened to need to visit the toilet after a board meeting and was positioned in trap two, when two of the director's came in to relieve themselves, their topic of discussion was how did 'that young upstart' (me) get away with dressing up like a yob to attend a board meeting? Also how does he listen to someone who hasn't got the cradle marks of his arse. I listened intently desperately trying to stifle a laugh. Wow what power they had just transferred to me, to use when they least expect it.

John King and I had a few disagreements in our relationship as Boss and subordinate, but the final encounter saddened me, it involved the same pricks at the urinal. I will relay this later at the end part of this section of my work career.

Chapter 25

Look confident and it will happen

There were many incidents that happened, and I always was in the right place at the right time, I had to go through some troubling situations, but managed to make the right decisions on the actions to take. Incident one was the third day of my arrival at the site. A lot of the managing directors of the individual Thorn companies on the site, were trying to make a name for themselves, in the hope of securing top jobs in the organisation.

At the beginning of my early days, I was, summoned by telephone to meet with the managing director of one of the companies on site. This was to attend an urgent meeting about a problem on a processing system. This problem was costing the company a large amount in losses of production, all caused by the lack of ability of the works engineering department, headed now by yours truly.

The problem I had, was that the tanks excavated to eventually house the plating processes, were leaking badly because no one accounted for the level of the local river (Lea), which rose significantly in heavy rain periods, putting a massive pressure on the concrete seams. I was to take the insults about how useless the department was and all its past failures. I will not bore you with the details, sufficient to say I was taken far beyond my tolerance level and had two choices, get up and walk out assuring that I would sort it all out, even though I did not have a clue where to start. Or my preferred approach, attack with both guns blazing. You have guessed right; I chose option two.

My reply was 'I do not know who you think you are, or who you think you are talking to, but from here it looks like you know zero about the problem your company has and far less about who you are talking to. I have been here three days and already met a person who thinks his surname is his title and a bunch of shop stewards who think they are going to dictate how my department works, both have deluded themselves. I run this department my way until someone has the courage to sack me, or I decide to tell the King to shove it up his arse. So, here is your choice, we work together on the problem, or you take me on, and the problem will never be resolved in my time. I can assure you of that.

I had calculated correctly and working together,

myself and Bill (the demi-God), solved the problem within a week, saving the company a lot of money. Bill became a main board member and features at the end of this section, one of the very few people I respected in my working life.

Friday came and I was greeted in the morning by the four shop stewards who wanted to discuss the overtime situation with me and when my secretaries were going to come back from the strike. Still working on how to solve the problem with the tanks, I was less than keen to have any meeting with the fantastic four, as I named them. But all part of the job so in they came, as usual I had not prepared anything, I was never one to do that, my temperament did not seem to allow for that.

The main mouthpiece a guy called Downer began with his list of men working on the weekend, my reply was 'you're on selective strikes and work to rule, there is no overtime.' I wished I had a camera to capture the complete surprise the four of them showed. 'What? That is impossible, production can`t work without works engineering being in.' Downer replied. I answered with, 'half the production shift are on strike, so 50% of the machines are not in operation, so we can afford to lose 50% of the machines before we affect the available production output. In fact, it is a perfect time to see what percentage of machines require attention on the weekend shifts, it could save our overtime bill, there is always a positive to be found in negativity'. You could have cut the atmosphere with a knife, Downer and two of the remaining three turned around without a reply and walked out of the office. The third, a steward for the AEU, a large boilermaker faced me across the desk and began by saying. 'You, young university boys think you are so clever you deserve a good hiding, messing with people's lives.'

I tried desperately to control the darkness that began to invade my thoughts I tried not to show my anger and replied as controlled as I could. 'Ok well firstly I am not a university boy, I went to a secondary school and did an apprenticeship in the dockyard. I have just been lucky, but if you want to teach me a lesson, I must tell you that I am a Judo expert, so when you end up at the bottom of the stairs to the workshop. You have been warned, do you agree?' I had already picked the spot for the first blow and the old feeling was increasing in momentum. He turned, head bowed and walked out of the office and down the stairs. I sat taking deep breaths until I was calm, so it was still there within me, the self-destruction trigger, more controllable but never far away.

Eventually the immediate industrial dispute got a resolution. At that time, the various trade unions were finding new ways of having as much control over companies as possible.

The favourite route at that time was health and safety. My problem was I had five of the shop stewards working for me. I struggled on with the cooperation between myself and the self-appointed safety co-ordinators (shop stewards), who often tried to interfere with my decisions, just to disrupt and challenge my authority. I had my bad days where I struggled to hold in my anger, but luckily, I had appointed an assistant works Engineer after George had retired due to his heart problems. Peter was dependable and managed to calm me down when he could see I was about to explode. Along with this situation with unions, rife back then, we had a couple of new appointments at senior levels, one being a guy who I named the tailors dummy, he dressed well and had extraordinarily little else to offer. He spent much of his time trying to get me to accept the shop steward's safety recommendations, without much success. Shortly after his appointment we began a re-organisation of the complete site, this was to remove two of the companies to the second main location at Cambridge Road in Enfield and to close half of the site, reorganising the remaining companies, the value of the project was around £3,000,000.00.

The project was to be co-ordinated by a consultancy company, with me in control of all the works, our site engineers, site security and contractors. What follows was unbelievable but true.

Firstly, when the guys from the consultancy company arrived, they insisted that they should have a meeting with all the shop stewards on site, to explain their brief and responsibilities on site, including their site rules and regulations, redundancy numbers included in the downsizing. Big mistake and the mistake of the senior site managers, as no one had discussed the personal situations of their members with the shop stewards. Last in first out was the order of the day.

The four guys arrived at around 10am on the Monday and were put into a dedicated ground floor office. Although my responsibility was also for site security, and building allocation, Tailors dummy, because of his special relationship with the shop stewards, took it upon himself to pick the only office with top opening windows and a single door entrance.

The site meeting was arranged in the front site entrance area and the owner of the consultancy company announced the procedures, redundancy numbers, payment basis and the statement that they would have full control over the departmental reorganisations. There was a stunned silence, I must admit I did not understand what they were talking about. Redundancies were the responsibility of the section managers in discussions with the union representatives and the personal department as it was called back then.

The four guys folded up their papers turned around and went back to their appointed office building. We all looked at each other and one of the shop stewards said in a very loud voice, 'over my dead body'. We all dispersed back to our various workplaces, Peter said to me 'what was all that about'? All I could answer was, 'I haven't got a clue, God help us.'

This was a troubled time there was a lot of unrest in the work forces, particularly with the miners and even amongst their own families. They caused everyone in the UK great hardship, apart of course, from the well off middle and high classes, which later to come to light, encompassing the politicians and miners leaders, deciding on how much misery the general public had to endure without even a vote on what they thought of the situation. Much the same as the decision to go into the Falklands. This was never officially recognised by UK or Argentina, as a declaration of war, but split a lot of families on their take on the situation and its rights and wrongs. Just to re-cap.

On April 2, 1982, Argentina invaded the Falklands Islands, a British colony since 1892 and a British possession since 1833. Argentina always wanted sovereignty over the Island, so sent amphibious forces to overcome the small garrison of British marines at the town of Stanley on East Falkland. The next day seized the dependent territories of South Georgia and the South Sandwich group.

The 1,800 Falkland Islanders, mostly English-speaking sheep farmers, awaited the British response. For those not familiar with the Falkland Islands they are located around 300 miles off the southern tip of Argentina.

It was the believed to be the British navigator

John Davis who sighted the islands in 1592, and in 1690 British Navy Captain John Strong made the first recorded landing on the islands. He named them after Viscount Falkland, who was the First Lord of the Admiralty at the time.

In around 1764, French navigator Louis-Antoine de Bougainville began the islands' first human settlement, on East Falkland, which was taken over by the Spanish in 1767. But In 1765, the British settled in West Falkland, but the settlement left in 1774.

Spain then abandoned its settlement in 1811, both believed to be uneconomical to keep the territory.

In 1816 Argentina declared its independence from Spain and in 1820 proclaimed its sovereignty over the Falklands. The Argentines built a fort on East Falkland, but in 1832 it was destroyed allegedly by the American ship, the USS *Lexington* this in retaliation for the seizure of seal ships owned by American companies in the area.

In 1833, a British force expelled the remaining Argentine officials and began a military occupation.

In 1841, a British lieutenant governor was appointed, and by the 1880s a British community of around 1,800 people on the islands was independently supporting its colony.

In 1892, the Falkland Islands were collectively granted colonial status, and for the next 90 years, life on the Falklands remained much unchanged. There were however persistent diplomatic efforts by

Argentina to regain control of the islands.

In 1981, the Falkland Islanders were given a referendum and voted to remain British. Meanwhile, in Argentina, the military junta led by Lieutenant General Leopoldo Gualtieri was, as by any dictator ruling with oppression. It was alleged he planned the Falklands invasion as a means of promoting patriotic feeling and propping up its regime.

In March 1982, Argentine salvage workers occupied South Georgia Island, and a full-scale invasion of the Falklands followed on April 2.

Under orders from their commanders, the Argentine troops inflicted no British casualties, which probably stopped the declaration of war. Britain was however outraged. A naval task force of 30 warships was assembled to retake the islands. As Britain is 8,000 miles from the Falklands, it took several weeks for the British warships to arrive. But on April 25, South Georgia Island was retaken, and after several intensive naval battles fought around the Falklands, British troops landed on East Falkland on May 21. After several weeks of fighting, the large Argentine garrison at Stanley surrendered on June 14, ending the conflict.

Britain lost 256 lives and five ships in the fight, Argentina lost its only cruiser and 750 lives.

Argentine military was swept from power in 1983, and civilian rule was restored. In Britain, Margaret Thatcher's popularity soared after the conflict, and her Conservative Party won a landslide victory in the

1983 parliamentary elections. However, the conflict caused much division even within families, as well as political and human rights groups. It showed how easy it was to divide people, when the true facts are not presented clearly and concisely to everyone involved.

We continued with our meetings as we were in the middle of budgets and re-organisation plans, but none of the information was disseminated to the individual groups of workers by the site management. Our planning office was positioned right in the far corner of the site, well away from the workshop, positioned by the consultants to allow as much privacy when they had their meetings with us.

Peter went out to get us a coffee, when he returned, he looked a bit bemused, I asked him what was wrong he replied that the workshop was empty even the storeman was missing. Like magic my telephone rang, and it was Gerry the personnel Manager. He sounded as if he was in a panic, Keith can you come over right away he asked, everyone is surrounding the room with the consultants in, they are panicking I have been over, but the men told me to fuck off or I would have the shit kicked out of me, what can I do help me please Keith,

Kings not here neither is Rodgers it is like they all disappeared. He sounded like a small child and without a clue what to do. 'Well, I answered they obviously decided to let the consultants cock it up before they did. Someone else to blame. Ok sit tight peter and I will be over.' 'Come on I said to Peter, don't rush, let them sweat it out for a while it will do them good'. As we approached you could only see a massive crowd shouting and waving their hands in the air. Luckily, my guys were at the back so I shouted, 'Right all works Engineering personnel still here in five minutes will be sacked, take this as a first warning anyone dismissed will not get redundancy money, so move your arses now.

Even now I will never know why they all took notice and although I was called some unpleasant things, every one of them headed back towards our works area, seeing these people leaving must have somehow triggered a thought that the demonstration was over and people began drifting away, I suppose it helped that 90% of my staff were male and the majority left were women.

As they drifted away just a hardcore of about ten men remained one of them being the most militant shop steward and usually the ringleader of any trouble on site. He stepped towards me and said, 'so what are you going to do?' I could feel the darkness beginning to descend, I had to control it, 'Nothing' I replied. 'Too many of us for you are there, we could give you a good hiding wimp.' He continued. That was simply perfect I travelled back to my school days history repeating itself. 'That's right they could, but you will never see what happens, or anything after that, I can promise.' The men behind him understood exactly what I ment, they then began to disperse, and he turned to follow them, he of course had to have the last word, all he could muster was, 'next time.'

I looked at Peter and all he could say was, 'need a wipe down?' 'No, I replied, but I think they might.' As we headed towards the door there was no sign of the personnel manager. I knocked and shouted, 'Ok open up its Mr Perkins, fun`s over you can go home.' The door was unlocked from the inside and then opened by the senior consultant very slowly.

'What the hell was that all about' he asked, still a little shaken. I told him I was not sure but thought it might be that they had heard there would be a lot of redundancies, due to the reorganisation of the site, which their company oversaw.

The project was directly from the new Managing Director, which I of course new nothing about. But as I was keen to discover what was going on I made a few guesses as to what was happening.

The King was being moved elsewhere within the refurbishing period, set as one year. All planned without any reference to me, this could explain the heart attack George had. The most interesting thing then, was I knew far more than the new senior management thought I knew. What follows was a classic situation borne out of pre-awareness and the fun of all the major players not realising the implications of underestimating someone having prior knowledge due to being at the right place at the right time.

Chapter 26

The king loses his crown

The first task before the presentation of the new site plans and reorganisation of the operation departments and buildings staying on site. Was to amalgamate the Staff and senior management canteen with the workers canteen. Yes, way back then managers and blue-collar worker groups sat in different areas. Now I was one of the senior management team, so got to eat in the same area as the King and his cronies (the other directors). He of course sat at the top of the table with two seats either side of him (for the four directors in favour at any given time). The two tables at each end and at right angles to the top table were for the occupation of the rest of us manager plebs.

Following the demolition of the dividing wall between the two canteen areas opening the horrific sight of plebs eating and drinking, came the announcement of Mr Kings movement to a new position at a different site.

Just think of the scene before this announcement, the daily struggle of power between the four directors desperate to get one of the two available seats each side of the King. The successful two hung on his every word, I enjoyed every session that I was present, just to see this adoration of someone I thought was a prick.

Then in a matter of days the top five seats (still in that configuration, be it free for anyone to take) were being occupied by the remaining directors, and his majesty was seated alone on one of the side tables. I must admit I felt a little sorry for him. I now reported to the new site Managing and Financial Directors and was now treated warily by the famous five. So, I sat next to King and could not resist the question, 'so where are your friends now John? they used to fight to sit next to you.' The sad thing is he looked at me straight in the eyes and replied. 'You don't realise, because you don't want to believe, people only ever use you for what your power can give them, nobody respects you for how powerful you are.' I couldn't resist it, so I replied, 'People only ever respect you if you deserve it, power is short lived without respect for others.'

That was the last time I saw him, as he got up and walked out of the canteen, briefcase in hand, head bowed. How the mighty fall, so with that the final part of my passage of time at Thorn`s, re-named,

Thorn EMI.

My best one upmanship ever and proof if I ever needed it, that someone or something was always close to me.

Chapter 27

Beginning of the end

The King had gone, I was informed, by my new managing director, that I was to collaborate directly with him and the site financial director, to control the large budget for the refurbishment and reorganisation of the companies on site.

That being the case I still had to report directly to the site manager, on all aspects of my department. I had aptly nicknamed him, tailors dummy abbreviated to TD. He dressed well and was as thick as a dummy as far as anything else went. It sounds good but, it was difficult for me because under TD I had to deal with the shop stewards, now deeply involved with the health and safety regulations now imposed by our government to protect the workforce. Some regulations desperately needed, others impossible to work with and in need of re-structuring.

Dealing with the first situation. A clear example

of taking over complete control due only to extraordinary situations.

I was called into the financial directors' office and was given my instructions on the handling of the project financial control. To protect me and for no other reason I was to select the list of three contractors for every job to be given. From these lists the financial director himself would vet the company and issue the contract to his chosen company.

I tried to explain with as much tact as I could muster, this was impracticable, some spheres of ability did not even have three companies capable of exercising the required operation.

His answer was, I was only young and some of these companies may be desperate to secure the contracts and I could be put in a position where I would be offered money in exchange for the contract. Although he would never dream that I would accept such an offer It was far safer to be seen to have all the contracts vetted by him.

I must admit that for the first time ever I was shocked that anyone would even contemplate I would do that, my interest was to get the job done the best and most efficient way. I had even changed a core heater at nine hundred degrees centigrade, with our chargehand to save production losses.

My reply was that I would think of the situation over the weekend and discuss the situation on the Monday. When I got home, I discussed it with Jackie, and she thought it was a bit of a cheek, but if it made the job slower it was their own fault. I was still not happy. We decided to take the children to the seaside on the Saturday to get it off my mind, then look at it on Sunday to work out the best way to present a way forward on Monday.

This next part takes a bit of time to believe it really happened. We arrived at the coast and parked up in the road overlooking the sea, yes you could park on the roadside then, without a parking charge. We had a wonderful time and later, I decided to walk along the road to the ice-cream kiosk and get us some cones. As I walked past the group of houses overlooking the sea, I suddenly saw the new managing director's car in the driveway of one of the houses. Even more odd, next door was the car of the partner of the group of consultants re-organising our site works and personnel redundancies.

I of course took a photograph of the situation and on our return home, had a lengthy discussion with Jackie on what I should do. She always told me to keep calm as that was when I was at my best and did the most damage to the opposition. So, I formulated my actions for Monday morning.

I was keen to get on, so I was waiting when Tom the Financial Director arrived, his secretary brought us both a coffee in and he sat back in his seat and began. 'Well Keith did you consider all the things we discussed on Friday?' 'Yes, I replied, I have a big dilemma, since there is a colossal amount of resentment on this site, towards the management, due to redundancies and company closures. Wouldn't it appear inappropriate for the unions to discover that one of the partners of the consulting company is the next-door neighbour of our managing director?'

His reaction was one of complete devastation rather than total surprise, confirming that he obviously knew the situation and had no understanding of how I knew this fact. I continued without looking concerned at all, 'Obviously this could be viewed that the Company will get a better service from the consultants, being as they will be in constant contact with our MD. Also, as I am the only outsider to know, to be trusted with this information proves that I can be totally trusted with exercising my responsibilities on contracts, without the need to interfere with decisions on contractors, which would waste both our time, and could cause me to doubt decisions on reasons to use contractors that I have not vetted, as part of my job'.

His reply was virtually inaudible, 'I agree it would be over the top for us all attempting to control the contracts on site, the consultants are on site to present the proposals on the site alterations and Management strategies for the new corporate Groupe, day to day operations will be under your direct control.'

I replied with the fact that this was much more efficient and will stop any conflicts in the control of contractors. We parted on the best of terms. Setting the bar from the outset is always best, even if you do not have a clue how you arrived at the solution by a chance encounter with an ice cream stall and two neighbouring houses.

The rest of the work went well, and the transformation of the site layout went exactly to schedule, both time and budget. We found the only problems caused were by the union representatives' insistence, on controlling the final health and safety regulations, on everything that was to be installed or moved in or out of the site.

This was a continuing annoyance to me, and I knew I would not be able to endure the complete subservience of the site manager to the shop stewards. It reached an impasse when the shop stewards insisted on stopping the delivery trucks and checking all the documentation on every visit. I lost it and told TD that I was revoking all shop steward interventions and anyone trying to continue would get written warnings leading to dismissal, meaning that their eventual redundancy pay would be zero. They of course went berserk, and TD had no clue how to manage the situation. So, I was invited to his office and told to think how we could get round the situation. That said it all to me, a clueless individual manager controlling a clueless bunch of no-nothing individuals. I turned around and left his office, walked over to my office, and told my secretary I was going home and taking the next day, which happened to be a Friday, off.

I then rang a friend of mine who ran an employment agency and asked him if he had a suitable job position on his books close to my home area. His surprising reply was yes last interview the next day (Friday). I went to the interview, and I received an offer of the job the same evening, starting in four weeks at the exact same salary as Engineering Manager with an American owned Company.

I of course accepted and arrived at the Brimsdown site on Monday morning, and I was greeted by Norma my secretary and told that TD was frantic to get hold of me as the unions were outraged at my refusal to accept their input.

I smiled at her and asked if she would type out my resignation letter for me? She could not believe it was true and thought it was just my brinkmanship tactic that I had used before, again I smiled and reminded her, you can only use that once, the second time it must be real. I saw a tear in her eye, we had become close friends, in a professional way, in fact she was only a couple of years younger than my mother and her husband Doug was an Engineer as well, so knew the pressures of unions in those days, thanks for Thatcher. Unfortunately, the battle became a war, and the country was again divided, the Miners were exploited by their leaders and allowed because of their methods to be divided in their ranks and destroyed, the classic divide and conquer and the

Union leaders couldn't see it coming.

So off I went with my letter in an envelope, I knocked on the door and heard the command 'enter.' there sat TD behind his impressive, polished desk with the usual lamp and calculator positioned in a symmetrical positioned either side of the leather blotting paper pad.

'Keith where have you been' he exclaimed. 'Well, I replied I took Friday off to consider the situation with the union shop stewards, and decided you were right, they should have the option of controlling the situation by using health and safety as a priority.'

His face visibly relaxed and the very next set of words that came out of his mouth were said in a joyful and in control tone, relaxed enough for the killer blow to have the full desired effect. 'So, what made you change your mind?'

'Because you will be controlling them, the best of fucking luck' I slammed the resignation letter down on the blotting paper pad, looked him directly in the eyes and in my head thought the next casualty. I turned and walked out to complete silence. This era was one of the battles, battles between Unions and the Government, and amongst the worst, with the miners.

The miners were defending their livelihoods and communities against the closures of the pits, and it was believed, the final confrontation, was a planned operation to crush the strike. Assault, lying under oath, perverting the course of justice became classed as serious criminal offences. It was planned to charge miners with riot, a charge which carried a potential life sentence, if police thought that the circumstances justified it. The first line of this paragraph, similar to taking a walk during the start of the invention of the lock up (softened by the use of the word Lock Down) simple manipulation of words. How gullible we were.

In a report to the South Yorkshire County council police committee on 25 September 1985, Peter Wright Chief constable, explained the decision was made, and a team of detectives appointed to collate evidence, following police officers' reports throughout May 1984 that miners were picketing violently at a place called Orgreave.

Discussions took place involving the chief constable, his senior staff, and the county prosecuting solicitor, who wrote. 'The chief constable decided that the usual charge of disorderly conduct, was inadequate and that appropriate charges of unlawful assembly should be preferred.'

On 18 June 1984, around 8,000 miners assembled for a mass picket called by the NUM and its then president, Arthur Scargill. South Yorkshire police claimed that 4,500 officers from different forces nationwide were there to police the coking plant.

Miners have always described their surprise they were not turned away by police that day, as was common during the year-long strike. They were allowed to assemble close to the plant, before being ushered into a large field, where police were massed at the bottom. A striking miner, called it a trap.

A West Midlands officer who served at Orgreave in a short shield police support unit (PSU), told the Guardian he believed the plan was to inflict a significant defeat on the miners:

It would have been easy to turn people away, but the decision was taken to let them in. If there was to be a confrontation, the police were going to win. The police account, both in the media on the day and during the trial the following year, was that the miners, unprovoked, had attacked police lines with sustained violence, throwing a continuous barrage of stones, and bottles, lengths of wood, metal objects and bricks. One miner, Russell, was filmed on television being beaten by a policeman just in front of the police lines. He was knocked over by a horse, he worked at Houghton Main colliery near Barnsley. He was then hit with a short shield, hit by a policeman, and attacked by another two as he was getting up. The police were out of control, and nobody has ever been held to account for what they did.

Much the same as has happened when people were protesting at the abuse of women by police during the drempt up pandemic used to control us all and divide people. Where Some were punched and kicked, and how many more raped, we know of at least one that was killed. As others were led through the police ranks, some were hit others dragged along the ground. Nothing changes.

Back to Work during the times of Thatcher, I had to give four weeks' notice of leaving, so I knew I had enough time to complete all the outstanding contracts, but of course he did not know that I could almost sense him behind me itching to get up to the MDs office and exonerate himself for any connection with me leaving.

On my final day I got a visit from Bill who was now a main board director, asking me what I wanted to keep me at the site. He knew what my answer would be, so he gave me a friendly punch to the stomach, wished me luck and drove off in his chauffeur driven Rolls Royce without visiting the other directors, including the site MD, who was watching from his office window.

My workforce had a leaving party for me and gave me a fishing rod and reel, and a farewell speech that was for me perfect and all I ever wanted to hear.

'Well Mr Perkins I must say that you have pushed us to our limits, in fact you have been a Bastard, but you have been a fair Bastard.'

I thanked them for their present and in reply said, 'I only hope my next set of workers are half as good as you lot and there are no fucking shop stewards in amongst them'.

I then turned my back on London, no more spending hours of wasted time in traffic jams, closed roads, accidents, arseholes that should have been permanently banned from driving. Hello to congested local roads, packed airports, strikes by baggage handlers long flights, delayed arrivals, lost baggage.

Well, what is the point of making a change unless it is different? Mind you I left a few useless individuals in senior positions only to gain more of them, although much fewer and less old school types.

Chapter 28

Beginning of another experience

I must say though my first day introduction to the new Company, was unusual, as it ended with one of the four senior managers giving me a year before he would get rid of me, as he could encompass my job as well as his own. My reply was immediate, back then I always had an answer, I would give him nine months, I gave him too much credit, he lasted just six Months. I wildly overestimated his ability.

This was a new adventure entirely, the equipment at this company was chemical dosing, measurement, and control. My missing element was chemistry, I had never studied chemistry and now I had a whole section of engineers both in UK and USA answering to me. The ones in USA had a manager who was a qualified chemist, so now I had to study to get to at least his level to be able to even understand the equipment. Had I at last taken on too much? Then how do you discover your limits until you assess them.

By now we had three children Mathew, Rebecca, and Danial our youngest. This job was going to be worldwide as the company had offices or representatives worldwide this was going to be the biggest challenge of my career and will put a strain on Jackie as I recognised that I would have to travel extensively. But as always, she was fully supportive of my decisions and I knew she would be able to cope with everything, how lucky was I to have that support, I could never have done it with anyone else, I am sure.

So, after meeting everyone and getting to know the people working for me, I was booked to travel to head office to meet with the senior members of the company. The company was in Colmar Pennsylvania. This was the first time I had travelled to America, and everyone came to see me off.

I had begun the most exciting period of my working life. It would be boring to go into the details of this next phase of my journey in life, but from the very beginning I had a protection of some strange Prescence that gave me an uncanny ability to see things in people and situations that were far beneath the superficial exterior signs.

I studied the chemistry topics that enabled me to understand what the complete process was about, and coupled with my formal qualifications, resulted in promotion during reorganisations within the ownership of the Company, to Engineering Director.

As I mentioned previously, the Sales Manager lasted for six months only, due to a letter from him to the American owners at the time, about the MD and his failings, ending up being left on my desk, which I accidently opened before I noticed it was on top of other letters, addressed to the sales engineers. This letter somehow found its way to the MD`s desk.

His actual intention was to get the position of Managing Director, instead of concentrating on me, he decided to initially go for the top position, using my engagement as part of the strategy. Unfortunately for him, my eagerness to learn chemistry from the chief chemist at the head office in America, was his biggest undoing, as he had also included detrimental comments about the chemist in his letter. What a tangled web you weave, when first you practice to deceive.

It is strange how a lot of people use a negative approach to life instead of using their positive abilities to achieve.

I made some good friends whilst working at this company, one of them whom I employed as one of my development engineers, ended up, and still is my business partner. As usual my inability to tolerate arseholes let me move on. This was a build-up of incidents beginning with the selling and re-structuring of the company through private equity. This could be a story in itself, but I will be brief.

It began with a meeting in Pennsylvania at a Hotel where the President, Engineering, Financial and sales, vice Presidents Plus the Head of the investment company, financing the buyout, were meeting with our team, The MD, Finance controller, sales manager, and myself (engineering manager). To discuss our positions within the new structure.

It became clear to me incredibly early on in the evening that there were no discussions, clearly the positions were already decided and who each of us were to report to. The only real negotiations were on salaries for each position. The only sticking points were the differentials in the salaries. Copious amounts of alcohol were easing this. Everyone apart from me was becoming drunk, mainly because three of the American board were modest drinkers, and in any case everyone apart from the head of the investment company, were staying in the hotel. Eventually everything was agreed and around midnight people began to go to bed. The investment guy decided he would drive home to Philadelphia, we tried to dissuade him, even to the point that Ron offered to let him sleep on the couch in his room.

He got quite aggressive towards Ron, so I said, 'let him go, he is a grown man, you're not responsible for his actions,' Ron replied, 'what if anything happens to him'. I flippantly replied, 'then he's dead.' With that he was already at his car and off he went, speeding out onto the main road.

The following morning, we all met at the dining

room for breakfast, during the breakfast there was a telephone call, and we were informed that the very person that Ron had tried to protect had driven off a bridge and was killed, apparently no one else took part in the incident. Ron like me has never forgotten the incident. But unlike me blamed himself for a long time for not insisting he stayed. I just thought, one less arsehole.

Eventually it was clear that the now part owners of the company were, as they always were incompetent and after various incidents the final inevitable incident happened, and I left the Company.

This incident may give some Insight into the minds of the type of person who seem to end up in positions of power, without any idea of how to react to situations or understand the people they oversee.

Being now Technical Director of the UK branch and development Director of the main Company. I managed future developments in the industry. One of these developments, I decided was ground-breaking, we designed and built a unit that did everything an expensive unit of one of our competitors did, but at one third of the price and most importantly a completely different concept, so patentable. Off I went to America with my star development project ready to present to the board. Just to prepare you for the type of minds that were in control of a specialised sector of essential services to world health and coupled with controlling the impact of the equipment on the environment.

I had already received a miss World style sash holding the words. The world's best development engineer. You can imagine my words which ended in, you can stick this up your arse. So, the end to an encounter I will describe later, will not come a surprise.

All the time my actions were taken, not entirely on experience, sometimes I had the same feelings that I had experienced in my childhood and youth, an inner voice or feeling that guided me to do things that came unexpectedly, not based on any clear path or information, just the inner feeling that I had way back when I was a child. I still felt the presence of that dark shadow that forced me to react instantaneously without any real regard of the possible consequences of those reactions.

Just a simple example was a visit to Hungry with the Managing Director to see our representative who also was part of the local government. Everything went well and we had the final night in a large hotel in Budapest. The incident began early in the evening. Frank and myself were in the bar at opening time, he like me enjoyed a drink, the music was playing, and we were approached by two young ladies, they were quite forward and after some banter about dancing, the girl talking to me said, 'You like me? You can have me 100 dollars, although I was quite taken back by her directness, I replied, 'No thank you, you can have me for 50 dollars, thinking this was a smart thing to say and would put her off, unfortunately it then became a banter of bargaining a price and ended up with an offer to me for 25 dollars. I laughed and said, 'No thankyou I never pay for sex.' She looked as if this never happened before to her, in fact she looked hurt rather than annoyed.

Getting back to the development project, it began with my presentation to the four Main board directors and became clear to me that nobody had a clue what I was presenting, but it did, as they say in the USA, violate something in their portfolio and this was their main field of focus, not the benefits to the environment or even the enhanced profits to the Company.

All they needed to do, was to explain to me that all the patentable development projects needed to be presented by the Main board Engineering Director and named as the developer. I would not have had a problem with that.

After some confused comments I was told we would re-convene in the morning as they had a board meeting scheduled within the next hour, I thought, my arse is a lemon, clearly, they needed in their heads (which contained shit), to devise some strategic reason why a development that would have given the company a position of technical superiority and enhanced environmental credentials. Should be discounted. So here goes with the best solution that they could produce.

The next morning, I was summoned to see the

President. A Guy called Reding. It was a nice morning, and I was invited to take a stroll in the grounds (car park), where he proceeded to relate an incident to me, featuring his daughter, this is remarkably interesting and may give some insight into the mind of a President of a Company in the USA, or anywhere else in the World, and certainly without doubt, members of the UK Government.

He began with 'One day, in fact the day of my wife's Birthday, my young daughter presented her with a beautiful birthday card edged in lace. My wife was ecstatic with this gift, but on closer inspection she realised the lace was part of some curtains that were stored in her bedroom draw. This ment that the complete day was spoilt because we had to punish her for taking the curtains without permission.' So, although her intentions were good, she had to learn never to assume it was OK to take something without permission, even if that would spoil the reason for taking them in the first place. I was totally confused, what was he talking about? Seeing my confusion, he thought he had to explain the meaning of his pathetic little story, but he had a shock, I was ahead of his puny brain ability. So, I replied 'If you do not want the development because you think I would expect to have joint patent rights, you do not know me. So, you can stick this fucking job up your arse and good luck with the prick who does not know what atmospheric pressure is. (Another story not even worth sharing). The Engineering VP.

With that I went back to the hotel, packed my bags, and got a flight back to the UK the next day. I arrived, home, to the surprise of my wife. I explained everything that went on and after my explanation, said that she would have expected no less a reaction from me. I had a lot of regrets, I made a lot of friends, people in Hungry, former Yugoslavia, Germany, U.S.A, Russia, in fact most countries of the world.

To see the death and destruction of Yugoslavia a country I visited four times, was tough.

The former Yugoslavia was a socialist state, created after German occupation in World War two and a bitter civil war. A federation of six republics, brought together. Serbs, Croats, Bosnian Muslims, Albanians, Slovenes, and others under a comparatively relaxed communist regime. Tensions between these groups were successfully suppressed under the leadership of President Tito.

But after Tito's death in 1980, tensions re-emerged. Calls for more autonomy within Yugoslavia by nationalist groups led in 1991 to declarations of independence in Croatia and Slovenia.

The Serb-dominated Yugoslavia army lashed out, first in Slovenia and then in Croatia. Thousands were killed in the latter conflict which was paused in 1992 under a United-Nations monitored ceasefire. Bosnia, with a complex mix of Serbians, Muslims, and Croatians, was next to try for independence. Bosnia's

Serbs, backed by Serbs elsewhere in former Yugoslavia, resisted. Under leader Radovan Karadzic, they threatened bloodshed if Bosnia's Muslims and Croatians, who outnumbered the Serbs, broke away. Despite a European vote to advise for the move in a 1992 referendum, war was the final outcome.

Yugoslavian army units withdrawn from Croatia and renamed the Bosnian Serb Army, carved out a huge swathe of Serb-dominated territory. Over a million Bosnian Muslims and Croatians were driven from their homes in ethnic cleansing. Serbia suffered as well. The capital Sarajevo was besieged and shelled. UN peacekeepers were brought in, to broker peace but, these peace efforts to stop the war failed and the UN were humiliated, and the result was the death of over 100,000 people.

The war ended in 1995, after NATO bombed the Bosnian Serbs, the Muslim and Croatian armies made gains on the ground. An America brokered peace divided Bosnia into two self-governing entities, a Bosnian Serb republic and in August 1995, the Croatian army attacked areas in Croatia under Serb control and thousands flee from the area.

Following this both Croatia and Bosnia were fully independent. By then Slovenia and Macedonia had parted, Montenegro followed later. In 1999, Kosovo's ethnic Albanians fought Serbs in another brutal war to gain independence. Serbia ended the conflict beaten, battered and alone Muslim-Croat federation lightly bound by a central government.

I had two friends on the opposing sides in the bitter war, I have never been able to contact them since that bitter conflict. I do know that a lot of refugees were sent to far off places with no protection or consideration for their safety. Some ended up no better than if they had remained where they were. Parents with their children were sent to places like Libya, and although I had good experiences, I would not have taken my wife or children there as refugees, life was tough, and it would have been a fearful place for a child. I guess my only other regret at the time I left the company was, I told them what I wanted, to leave without disruption.

They at once agreed to the demands, the big lessen I had learnt for the future was, always ask for more than you ever expect possible to get. Learning all the time.

I left pretty quickly and decided we would have a holiday before I began deciding what I would do. The obvious solution was to go to Gerry, the recruitment Company owner who had set me up with the interview at Capital Controls. I relayed what had happened and asked what he had going. His reply was surprising but ended up one hundred percent correct. 'Keith, some people, are unemployable in the context of working for a large Company. You need to set up your own Company, or buy into an established one, I can't really help you in the long term.

I thanked him for his honesty and decided to contact a Company that I had dealt with and in fact had discussed the possibility of Capital Controls using their dosing pumps for liquid disinfection.

Chapter 29

Onwards and upwards

The Company was a distributer for a large dosing systems company in Germany. The UK branch was known as Jesco UK Ltd; this UK branch used pumps supplied from Jesco Germany, but that Company also produced the full range of products to directly compete with Capital Controls.

I organised a meeting with the two owners of the Company and got on very well with them. After the well-deserved holiday (in my opinion). We discussed all the possibilities and finally agreed that I would buy a third of the Company shares and would become the Technical Director of the Company.

We would expand the range of equipment and offer installation. Now the company would sell the full range of water disinfection equipment and become a direct competitor in the water and sewerage, dosing, and control sector.

We took the Company from a turnover of around £400,000 to around £1.5 million, winning projects in UK and eventually in Libya, Jordon, and USA.

Working with the water companies in the UK, I was able to re-design and improve equipment resulting in our company having our own products, which included controllers, special gas and liquid dosing systems and analysers.

At round, this time one of the people that worked directly for me at Capital controls decided he had also had enough at the old Company and started his own. I used him on a few of our developments and we worked very well together.

There are a few incidents in life that you will always remember exactly where you were, as I said before, in my life there have been more than one, this dramatic incident happened as I was driving home to my house in Gloucester, I was close to the turn off to the bridge crossing when my music was interrupted by a news bulletin. There had been an attack on the Twin towers in New York, by two commercial planes. I actually missed my turning, I couldn't believe what I was hearing.

It was September 11, 2001, P.M our time, morning in the USA, nineteen terrorists hijacked four Commercial airline planes, scheduled to travel from the east coast to California. The hijackers crashed the first two planes into the Twin Towers of the World trade centre in New York City, and the third into the Pentagon in Arlington County Virginia near Washington, D.C. A fourth plane was also intended to hit a federal government building in D.C. but crashed in a field following a passenger revolt. The attacks killed nearly 3,000 people and instigated the global war on terror.

The first impact American Airlines flight 11 was crashed into the North tower of the World Trade Centre complex in lower Manhattan at 8:46 a.m. Seventeen minutes later, at 9:03, the World Trade Centre's south tower was hit by United Airlines flight 175, bringing about the destruction of the remaining five structures in the WTC complex, as well as damaging or destroying various other buildings surrounding the towers. The third flight, crashed into The Pentagon at 9:37 a.m., causing a partial collapse.

The September 11 attacks, commonly known as 9/**11**, were four, coordinated suicide attacks, conducted by the militant Islamist extremists network al-Qaeda, against the United States. Whoever was ultimately behind it will probably never be known. The brave passengers of flight 93, attempted to gain control of the aircraft, but the hijackers ultimately crashed the plane in a field in Stony creek Township, Pennsylvania, near Shanksville, at 10:03 a.m. Investigators determined that Flight 93 was targeting either the United States Capital, or the White House.

Within hours of the attacks, the central intelligence agency determined that al-Qaeda was responsible. The United States formally responded by launching the war on terror. and invading Afghanistan to depose the Taliban, which had not complied with U.S. demands to expel al-Qaeda from Afghanistan and extradite its leader, Osama bin laden. Eventually assassinated.

There have been a lot of conspiracy theories about 9/11. Facts are still that the West sold and supplied the Afghanistan's who were in alliance with the Taliban, with weapons to defeat and expel the Russians from Afghanistan, the Taliban and al-Qaeda are effectively the same. And after all, before the end of this story Afghanistan are back to pre-the 9/11 days How? Why?

Back to the continuation of my story. Everything was going well for our newly formed alliance, Jesco UK Ltd. But like always I could never have an unchallenging ride through life, there always seemed to be a disruption that led to another change of experience, not just a simple progression, a dramatic incident that left no possibility but to make a change.

This time it was an unexpected situation with no chance of ever predicting it, or the outcome due to it.

Tony one of my two business partners, Joe being the other, was a little unpredictable, but was always on time for meetings and work. We began getting complaints from customers about late deliveries of equipment and sometimes deliveries of the wrong equipment to a site.

These mistakes were all on the equipment Tony oversaw. This particular day, we had communication from a customer complaining that equipment was outstanding but was informed by Tony that it had been dispatched a week earlier. I looked out into the workshop and there was the equipment all ready for dispatch.

The odd thing was Tony was now an hour late for work and I needed to check with him, in case there was a reason for the holdup. With that Tony appeared with an apology that he had woken up with a strange feeling and found it difficult to walk down the stairs from his bedroom, almost falling, he then could not coordinate his actions to eat his breakfast, so he rested and after a time everything was back to normal. He then told me he had difficulties coordinating the action of coming up the stairs to the office. I was genuinely concerned, as this had every sign of a stroke, even though he was only in his early thirties, a stroke can happen at any age.

I began to put together the incidents with the equipment deliveries, I persuaded him to go to the doctors and after many consultations he was finally diagnosed with a tumour at the point of the spine joining the brain and this was to be a life changing situation with no permanent positive solution.

This was devastating news for us all, Tony was a good friend as well as a colleague, but his deterioration was rapid, completely altering his personality. Joe and I had to hold the company together and the customers of course were only interested in the negative effect on their requirements for equipment and services. A lesson that there is no compassion in business, just opportunities from people's demise.

It is difficult to understand the dramatic devastation this type of situation has, customers in the chain have only one choice, to fulfil their requirements, so they go elsewhere, then when you are down and struggling to overcome, not only the loss of a friend and colleague, but the mayhem that has on the established business.

The sharks line up, the biggest predators being the banks. They never have and will never have, any regard for their customers or offer any help without gain. As if for some unknown reason to give Joe and myself no option to continue with our business, a rule was passed in New Zealand changing the situation of money liabilities of limited company owners and directors, in the favour, of loans from banks and it was also applied to businesses in the UK. I tried to argue the point through my then local Conservative representative.

He was as useful as a wet paper bag. I would have been better to have had a conversation with my dog, at least he listened, maybe that was because I was holding his favourite treat. I guess I may have done better if I could have presented a treat, to my local government MP back then, they seem to like treats.

So as usual I took on the fight myself. A

representative of our bank told Joe and me, in his words. 'Don't try to fight us we are so powerful and have so much money we can break you, you can never win.'

This was like a red rag to a bull, to me, my immediate reply was. 'Yes, but what if you lose against pleb`s like us? How many class actions will you face then, are you man enough to risk that, I only have a house to lose you have a job and reputation, and a massive bonus to lose and who will employ a big time looser.'

For whatever reason after a much different path of negotiations, we settled for fairer and realistic figure, and we kept our houses. I feel sorry for the ones who lost everything they had built up, on what was either an unsound financial law, or a new law dreamed up to cheat the Ltd company owners out of money by the banks. I often wonder if that law and decision. Obviously brought about by the greed of the banking fraternity. Had been questioned with the knowledge of the incompetence soon to be displayed by the banks, leading to them being bailed out by the people they cheated back then.

How many of those businesses would have been saved and still be contributing to the success of UK.

This encounter gave me so much more than a fair outcome, it gave me total loss of fear, of institutions that believe, we are insignificant plebs.

Never forget, many knowledgeable plebs become a powerful force with the ability to change situations for the better, class acts were few back then, and not every lawyer firm was capable of taking on a big corporation.

I had met a lot of interesting people, made a few lifelong friends and I hope, made a positive change within the industry, influencing changes on the design of equipment and control techniques. In fact, I sold systems into Libya with the help of our salesman John. Another of my interesting passages of time.

As ever I happened to be lucky to be in the right place at the right time. My first encounter was at the airport meeting a Kaddafi bodyguard with two other suited men. His dress was a long white robe and a head cloth. He approached me and stood directly in front of me, too close for my comfort, and stared into my eyes, I of course stared back, I was in my comfort zone, intimidation only heightened my senses.

He then held both my shoulders and kissed each cheek, then said 'we will be friends you are like me, no fear of death, only of life.' I did not really understand his words until much later on. He was right we did become friends and I learned a lot, some things near the final days of the Kaddafi regime I did not even dream could have been true until much later, when the world was turned upside down by democratic countries experimenting with the extents a dictatorship could be imposed.

A UK parliamentary report has severely criticised

the intervention by Britain and France that led to the overthrow of Libyan leader Muammar Gaddafi, the then PM David Cameron was accused of lacking a coherent strategy for the air campaign. It said the intervention had not been 'informed by accurate intelligence', and that it led to the rise of so-called Islamic State in North Africa.

The UK government said it had been an international decision to intervene. The action had been called for by the Arab League and authorised by the UN Security Council, the Foreign Office added. An international coalition led by Britain and France launched a campaign of air and missile strikes against Muammar Gaddafi's forces in March 2011 after the regime threatened to attack the rebel-held city of Benghazi. Yes, we sided with the rebels.

But after Gaddafi was toppled, Libya descended into violence, with rival governments and the formation of hundreds of militias, while so-called Islamic State, also known as Isil and Daesh, gained a foothold.

The committee's key conclusions include through his decision making in the National Security Council, David Cameron was ultimately responsible for the failure to develop a coherent Libya strategy.

The possibility that militant extremist groups would try to benefit from the rebellion should have been anticipated. It saw no evidence that the UK Government conducted a proper analysis of the nature of the rebellion in Libya. UK strategy was founded on erroneous assumptions and an incomplete understanding of the evidence, the limited intervention to protect civilians had drifted into an opportunist policy of regime change. That policy was not underpinned by a strategy to support and shape post-Gaddafi Libya. Political engagement might have delivered civilian protection, regime change and reform at lesser cost to Libya.

Mr Cameron defended his handling of the situation, telling MPs in January, action was needed because Gaddafi, was bearing down on people in Benghazi and threatening to shoot his own people.

But the foreign affairs committee said the government failed to identify that the threat to civilians was overstated.

The government failed to identify or accept the 'militant Islamist extremist element in the rebellion'.

MPs said that the possibility that militant extremist groups would attempt to benefit from the rebellion should have been recognised. More damming that the UK strategy was founded on assumptions without a complete understanding of the evidence available. This episode says it all, nothing dramatic, just twisting the truth or worse still genuinely not recognising the evidence in front of their eyes. Before this dramatic ending of a whole society, I was sitting with the bodyguard, discussing his role and how he got to be in the position. His answer was that they trained from an early age and only the best and most ruthless got through the training and given the position of bodyguard. They kept the position for as long as their challengers lost, most times the looser paid with their lives.

Their privileged positions ment that very few lived past their length of duty. I asked him why the West, including the UK along with USA wanted Kaddafi deposed, a statement he often made.

He replied without hesitation, because the colonel bought gold from the UK at a competitive price, because the UK was having huge economic problems. Then when it got better in the UK, they wanted to buy it back at the same price they sold it for. Kaddafi refused, so UK and USA decided they would get rid of him. The words of a trusted bodyguard, one that would be present at high level meetings. Of course, at the time there was no way I could believe that explanation. I still respected our government as a whole, although the individuals I did not respect were increasing in their numbers. Muhammad the gun, although on the surface a violent person, was in fact a lover of culture and took us to see some of the beautiful historical sites in his Country. I have included them here; I doubt that many people will have the chance to see them, which I think is a grate shame as people and their Countries are portrayed at their worst by the press, an unfortunate legacy of the world situation at this time.

Libya is a country with a varied past. It has been inhabited by Berbers since the late Bronze age. The Phoenicians established trading posts in western

Libya, and ancient Greek colonists established city-states in the east of the country. It had been ruled by Carthaginians, Persians, Egyptians, and Greeks. The entire region became a part of the Roman Empire. History has seen both Ottoman and Italian rule. The result of such a diverse history is a wealth of fascinating sites.

Leptis Magna later became part of the Carthaginian Empire and was then incorporated into the Roman Empire in 46 BC. Most of the remaining structures now found the site are Roman and originate from the reign of Septimius Severus. Among the many remains found in Severus' home city, are the marketplace, Severin Basilica, the Forum, the Amphitheatre, and the Severin Arch. They represent some of the best-preserved Roman sites in the Mediterranean.

Leptis Magna is an incredibly well-preserved archaeological site in Tripoli. Originally founded by the Phoenicians. The port of Logy in the first Cyrene in Libya, is considered to be one of the most impressive Greco-Roman sites in the world and one of the best Classical Greek sites outside Greece itself. Amongst its fantastic remains, Cyrene is home to the ruins of the great sanctuary of Apollo which has sites ranging from the Temples of Artemis and Apollo, which date back as early as the 7th century BC, to the 2nd century Trajan Baths.

One of its most impressive sites is Cyrene Amphitheatre, which the Greeks built in the 6th century BC, it was used as a Roman amphitheatre and is now the largest Greek site in Africa. There's lots more to see at Cyrene including its acropolis, agora, forum, and necropolis. Part of what makes Cyrene so incredible is not just its monuments but its overall planning, a mix of Greek and Roman, which is evident throughout. Sabratha, once a thriving Roman city, lay approximately fifty miles west of Tripoli, remarkably picturesque, the ruins of Sabratha look out across the Mediterranean and give visitors an insight into why this location served the ancient trading routes so well.

Much of what can be seen at Sabratha today was partially or wholly reconstructed by the Italians in the early 20th century, under Mussolini who gave speeches from the ancient theatre. Today, visitors can explore an impressive set of ruins, including the three-storey theatre, several temples, and the remarkable remains of luxury Roman villas, with well-preserved mosaics. Along with the Byzantine-era Basilica of Justinian.

The ancient oasis city of Ghadames lies close to the Libyan border with Algeria and Tunisia. The old town is a labyrinth of tunnels, houses, courtyards, and places of worship, all built underground to provide protection from the heat of the Sahara.

Today several houses of the deserted town have been furnished and restored to give the handful of visitors an idea of what they were like to live in. You can also travel across the rooftops as the local women once did.

The Arch of Marcus Aurelius was built around 165 AD in the city of Oea in Libya to celebrate the victories of Lucius Varus, who had defeated the Parthian Empire. The Capital city, Ctesiphon. Comprised of a central stone dome held by flat slabs, the arch was erected entirely of marble. The arch stood at the intersection of the city's main streets, dominating the route of travellers who would witness the triumphant might of the Roman empire. Today, the Arch of Marcus Aurelius is the sole remaining structure from Roman era Oea, although the arch itself is well-preserved.

Back to the meeting with Muhammad the gun, the actions to come in the future from this period of conversation, it is at least, clear that our governments are capable of any atrocity to gain control of the will of the people. Or crush people who deplore their tactics even though the majority of the people are just living day to day, some only existing.

On the Friday before Kaddafi went into hiding, Mohamed the gun called me, and told me I should be ready early on the Saturday morning, as I was to be sent back to the UK, on what was to be the last flight out of Libya.

I arrived home and Jackie had followed the situation in Libya on the television not knowing where I was. For my part there was no internet or telephone services to countries outside of Libya. She was rightly worried about me travelling to these types of countries. We successfully saw the return of the other UK workers from Benghazi via a ship.

This left me with a lot to consider as I was now aging and although I was still left with what I believe was a special insight, I could not predict how long it would last, or when it would stop, even if it was real. Was it just a figment of my imagination that would stop at any time, or worse I was just mentally unstable and had damaged my body and brain as a child.

I enjoyed pushing the boundaries of decisions in dangerous situations, it gave me a buzz, the more dangerous the situation the more satisfied I was when I got through it.

The same feeling of excitement and fear that I had, when the two blood red eyes stared down at me before the greatest pain I had ever had, followed by the euphoria of knowing that I had cheated death, not only death but had seen the eventual destruction of the cause of my real pain. No one knew my true secret. It was like a drug, I needed, to have challenging situations that were dangerous enough to cause that feeling of a fear. Strangely enough I think at least one of my sons has that similar self-destructive urge. If it is true, he will need to control it to get the best out of the moment, good luck, I still can't say I have any real lasting control, just the odd success.

I suppose the biggest problem was the lack of respect I had and still have for people that were or are in positions of power with no right to be there. I have met many of them in all levels of society, was it me, not them? Did I really expect them to recognise their level of incompetence when I did not even know my own? I have never believed that I will ever reach that point, how conceited.

Chapter 30

Chris and c.s.b

As I mentioned before Whilst at Capital Controls, I was good friends with one of my development Engineers, we first met when I decided I would start Judo, to give me a further confidence in controlling my aggression rather than regret my actions. The ironic situation is, he is ten years younger than me, and his birthday is one day before mine in the same month, so we are both Gemini's. It is sad to say that he was and is much better than me at Judo, I put it down to his ten-year age advantage not my lack of skill and control.

When I joined Jesco UK I continued to use his services on development, as he had formed a company himself. Eventually after a period of working as a self-employed person, doing work for various water treatment companies, I had an offer of a contract to develop a measurement and control system for a large chemical company in the UK. This was a remarkably interesting project because it was a new dosing media for sewerage disinfection.

Chris, as well as being OK at Judo, is a brilliant electronic development Engineer. I approached him with a proposal that eventually resulted in us becoming business partners.

As I explained above, I had a development proposal requiring innovative technology in dosing and control of an emerging water disinfection media. It ment that I had a retention by the chemical company to develop the measurement and control system, for the USA market.

We worked together on the new analyser system, using my process knowledge and his exceptional ability in electronics and control theory.

We eventually developed an analyser system that could accurately measure the residual chemical in sewerage or final effluent. Completion of the original task showed clearly that this chemical company was not equipment or systems orientated, and consequentially decided to put us in touch with two entrepreneurs both residing in Finland, who would develop the market for this system, agreeing to give first option on purchase of the chemical from this chemical company, the best option for all parties at the time.

The size of the cost to finance this project required funding so eventually the two entrepreneurs secured funding from a Russian owned company working out of Finland. CSB as our company was abbreviated to, were given a contract to develop the analyser part of the total system along with the engineers employed by the newly formed Company in Finland.

CSB, through my contacts, had already set up a dialogue with a chemical company in USA. We eventually signed a contractual agreement to supply and help with installation of the developed units.

Eventually the USA company wanted to expand into Europe and the Finnish company wanted to form an alliance in USA, so we received an offer by the Finnish company, a proposal to buy 30% of our shares, this proposal was agreed.

All this information, although boring needed an explanation, because it helps show my uncanny ability of seeing something in a situation that is not even apparently related.

The Finnish company due to many typically boring factors, were losing money and trying to re-finance, as they owned 30% of our company. They called a meeting with us to explain the situation and to tell us that they had met up with the chemical company's board to try to secure finance.

We were informed that we would have to work closer with the head of the chemical company section. If it did go through, ironically our distributer would have owned a third of CSB.

By luck or design, we had scheduled to have a three-monthly meeting with the chemical company the very next week in USA. As the Fin`s left the meeting I turned to Chris and said, 'Looks like there is a plot to eventually take over our company beginning with having a third of our shares. Who gets to be used you or me?'

Chris looked strangely at me and said, 'how do you get that? nothing was mentioned other than collaborating with them'. I just smiled and said, 'trust me, his eyes did all the talking, not his mouth, that just spouted bullshit.'

We arrived at the scheduled meeting in the USA, the office of this company was near the top floor in a high rise building along with many other companies. Typical of Philadelphia.

All the way up in the elevator Chris kept asking 'do you think we should mention this, what if you are wrong?' My answer was 'I am not wrong.'

We arrived at the meeting room and were informed the head of department, could not be at the meeting because she had to attend an emergency meeting elsewhere. I replied, 'That's OK but before we officially start our meeting I need a couple of answers to questions, that you may have to contact someone to give you the answers.'

As I expected he was eager to please us, giving me full confidence, I was right. 'Why are you trying to get our shares without prior discussions with us, or notification of discussions to be held with one of our major shareholders?'

His immediate answer was unexpected and naïve.

'It's not at due diligence.' Confirming their intention to take over the company owning our shares whilst holding a confidential non-disclosure distribution agreement with our company, without discussions.

Chris was shocked and even now still says he did not understand how I knew. My instincts always gave me a head start, most times that is all you need. The USA company pulled out of the situation; the Finnish company went bankrupt. We agreed a settlement in Finland resulting in us taking back our shares. Because of the pride of the American company, we also came to a financial agreement with them, which happened just prior to the so-called pandemic. This enabled us to further develop our products.

This was a strange time as my mother was taken into hospital at the age of ninety, she deteriorated quickly, luckily it was before the total collapse of the NHS caused by BATS???

We were able to visit my mother in her final days, soon after this period in time visits were stopped, leaving parents and their children separated by a wall of deceit, created by the new regimes formed around the world. My mother's last days were something I will never forget, but at least I was with her.

She had the chance to discuss a short story she had written to tell us about her life. In fact, she gave me the inspiration to write about my life. I eventually got to have the story, which I still have in its original form.

It was January 1936 when King George 5th died and Edward appointed King, at the same time my grandfather's health was getting bad and he could no longer work. My mother found out from a friend that my grandfather's funeral had already been planned. My mother was seven years old, and her brother eleven.

My mother was traumatised by her father's death and contracted a nervous complaint, known commonly as saint Vitus dance. She recovered and my grandmother remarried.

My step grandfather was a complete waste of space and eventually after making advances toward her, my mother moved in with her aunt and stayed with her until she was married in 1948, the year my wife was born.

We talked about my father, and how from the time of their marriage, he was only interested in his own needs. She always remembered the Christmas that he told her he had gambled away all his Christmas pay and would not have any more money until the end of January. She was beside herself with panic, left with no money, no presents, and no food. She was out of pure despair, forced to borrow money from my grandmother, who herself was married to a complete imbecilic moron.

What chance did she ever have of happiness. If I had known the full extent of his abuse, I would have made a different decision than to try to take my own life.

Getting back to my mother's revelations, it was my father that decided we would live with his parents, not of course a joint decision, but one to save him money, money he could then squander on gambling and women.

The sad truth is that my mother through her whole life believed she had protection by this entity she called God, when it was her who was doing all the protecting.

She sacrificed the whole of her adult life looking after us, her children and supporting a useless piece of shit who saddled her with the responsibility of looking after us all.

Where was this entity when she cried herself to sleep, not knowing that I could hear her sobs.

Her story continues through her life dedicated to the church, but when I eventually got the opportunity to read it, it confirmed to me that religion is nothing to do with a God. It is the quality of the people forming the congregation that support the parishes. God is a title given to the reason for unexplained happenings, good or bad.

Anyway, off we went to live at my grandparents' house. We took over the entire front room according to my mother. She confirmed that at this early time in their marriage, she suspected his lust of women was in the forefront of their life. In fact, she was even sure one of them was the daughter of the proprietor of the local pub, only a few doors down from my grandparent's house, ideal position from his chosen resting place. I am thankful that I was able to be by her side when she was, no longer able to even blink, she, in no more than a whisper, asked me to hold her. I am so pleased that I was able to as it was to be the last time I ever did.

When I think of all the people who never had that final closeness with the person that carried them inside their body, breathing together as one. Denied that final intimate moment, by a failing institute being held together by a bunch of bumbling idiots, supported by a paid list of idiots described by our government representatives as experts.

All, it must be obvious, supported by a media system designed to breed more fear into people, by issuing statements night after night using figures, which never made and still make no sense.

A bunch of lies drempt up by liars to justify the prevention of that final shared love between child and parent, husband and wife, brothers, and sisters. The excuse, lack of space, another lie. What happened to the special centre, the one that has added millions of pounds to the pocket of the foreign owner of property in our country? Then the final Insult, after all the restrictions and turning people against each other.

No emergence of a transformed health system, just continuing chaos. We should try changing the experts in charge. The problem is, can we trust anyone called an expert?

Things are so easily manipulated, below is just a

simple drawing with what appears to be, a meeting between my daughter and Brad Pitt, she adores him.

LOOK WHO I BUMPED INTO DAD!

Of course, it's just a joke between us drawn by me, an illusion, just like the `Pandemic` If you use the loose term, but was it? If you use the correct term, it was never proven to be more than an epidemic, just a play on words.

Getting back to my situation in the battle to keep our Company, allied to the hospital situation. One of the reasons to try to get an agreed settlement in USA, rather than face a court case, was a stroke I had. Jackie was convinced it was due to the pressures of this traumatic situation with the Company, who knows, all it did, is to confirm the strange operation of my body, all the standard signs were never present, even the hospital were surprised at the odd medical manifestations.

I thought it was food poisoning, which began with sickness on the aeroplane, travelling on a return flight from Rome, because of this, I did not contact the emergency service until well after 24hrs of what had to be the start of the stroke.

That day my transportation from the aeroplane to my car in the airport parking lot, was firstly in a wheelchair, and then an electrical carriage, which ironically features later in the story. I have to say the airline and the people at Gatwick were brilliant.

Finally on arrival at the hospital the emergency stroke team, at first, did not think it was a stroke and when the results of a CT scan confirmed it was, even they were surprised it was a complete blockage on the left-hand side.

I never lost speech and was just dizzy and sick. Without dwelling on the situation, the blood clot, had to eventually be chemically dissolved and I was discharged after only four days. Again, everyone involved in my hospitalisation were brilliant. The consultant gave me all the answers he could, one of them interested me very much as the new introduction of flu jabs had been introduced for us, older generation. My stroke was discovered, as being due to scoring inside my artery, causing the build-up of the material/proteins, this could not be explained, however in the light of the emergence of information sighting the extensive use of graphene (cell binding agent), in flue injections, if eventually proven to be true, could go some way to explain the situation. I believe there are extensive research into modifications to the structure of the binding agents using modified forms of the original binding agent.

I began having the flue injection one year before my stroke. My research into properties shows, Graphene is an allotrope of carbon consisting of a single layer of atoms arranged in a two-dimensional honeycomb lattice nanostructure. The name is derived from 'graphite' and the suffix -ene.

Graphene molecular make up is like small razor blades, which could easily score the inside of an artery or vein. Was graphene in its old formation used in early development of flue injections? Is it dangerous? I do not think we will ever know, honesty has never been part of dictatorship or democracy, today they are fast becoming one of the same. My interest is not and will never be to sue for money, but to make sure it is either modified or an alternative found. Nobody with an understanding of this development has ever asked me about my situation or interestingly enough not asked for mc to take a scan to see if the scoring remains or if it has repaired. It could give some useful data.

The interesting thing was when Chris and I set off to the meeting to decide if we proceeded to court or agreed a settlement as we left for the departure lounge to fly out, randomly a trolly stopped by the side of us and the driver asked if we would like a lift to the terminal as he was heading that way. We of course accepted, as we began moving off, I suddenly realised that this was exactly one year after my stroke and happened to be Friday the 13th. An omen? We settled out of court.

So where does democracy fail so badly? Simple, relying on people's ability to distinguish between the actual truth and the perceived truth. One of the recent mistakes by our government in power at the time, was giving the vote, known as the referendum, on leaving the EU to the people. There was no thought given on how to present the positives and negatives. Mainly because half the politicians didn't understand themselves.

This was not about freedom; it was given because the political parties knew the country was divided. The information given to explain the for and against was not clear. The message given was that we paid too much money to the EU, along with too many people from EU countries were moving to UK and claiming our benefits. None of these reasons were viable or materially sustainable.

The main reason was the inability of our politicians to negotiate the best deals for the UK to remain. All the rhetoric unfound but used in the end to mask the real truth behind the move. Prevent the unity of the people. It did not really matter which way the vote went. To stay ment the Conservative party remained as it was, with a small shuffle of politicians, to oust the reserve leavers.

To leave, slightly more complicated, a much larger re-organisation and an incredibly careful change in attitude of the stay candidates to convert to leave. Then of course it became politically messy, as it was such a close vote, it divided not only the people but the areas of the UK.

What did we need to divert attention from World politics and especially those in Europe? A disaster or two.

Let us ask another searching question. Why has no political party ever given a referendum on capital punishment?

This one is much more complicated as the final justification could conflict with the needs of the regime.

This could cause problems, as countries that are homes to such terrorists, work with and for the very Governments calling themselves democratic. The same regimes we have supported by our lack of action on capital punishment and deportation. Go back to the bad old days in this story, where did Amin come from? where did Isis recruit from?

What country would allow terrorists, in the full view of their protectors, the police, kill innocent people, and then put them in a comfortable jail to live out their lives paid for by the very society of people they have violated. Answer. The democratic countries housing those criminals.

As we now know the referendum, we were given would not disrupt politics, just a pre-curser to figure out the percentage split of people needed, to give the ultimate power to the democratic governments to allow then to create and assess tolerance of temporary dictatorship, and its length of sustainability.

The United Kingdom was an Ideal place for the test, a small area with the greatest diversity of people and cultures Firstly, allow division of Scotland, Northern Ireland, and Wales from England. Give them different rules to further divide them. Only the minority want it, but that's good, they are the ones willing to mouth off. The majority do the usual thing, bow their heads, and keep quiet, so you never know actually how many have the same views (majority).

Did you ever notice the reporters always show the same number of for as against, that's democracy. All carefully chosen to broadcast.

The amount actually asked, let's be generous 10 out of 55,000,000 Very well engineered by the BBC. Who of course kept the licence fee and had the greater number of the captive audience, whilst giving the same time to advertisements even though we still pay for a licence. Admittedly they only advertise their own programmes featuring men kissing men, products, promotions, without of course considering the majority of their paying customers.

Chapter 31

Test for democracy

Create a worldwide disaster, and what better than one caused by a wild creature, it has already been evaluated and found effective, innocent, and free of any political incentive.

A rapid response of most of the free world Countries known as the G20 joined quietly by all the world leaders. Blame it on the BATS.

The World now has a Pandemic, caused by a creature that occupies vast areas around the world. But how will people believe this? Involve a viral test facility in a Country known by most people in the world as one run under a Dictatorship. We give you the Coronavirus Pandemic, which embraces every country in the world, and all within just a few weeks?

Why? Because whenever control of the people is demanded, Democratic Countries can now claim the right to introduce the rules of dictatorship. In most cases rules set by a government given power by a small majority, of the small number of citizens that bothered to vote. Nevertheless, in a democratic society this gives ultimate authority to a minority.

But even worse, in our beloved Country, that minority can change their leader, even without the people who voted for that party, having any input.

With the collective power of the G20 all governments of the 'Free World' could control the democratic world, using the well proven tactics of dictatorship, one being the use of the news media.

Of course, every country will vairy slightly and focus on various aspects of control, but the core elements of their strategy will be transparent. Climate change, control of travel, reducing cross communication, manipulation of resources, to control the revenue to oil and gas rich countries. There must be the odd engineered disagreements between the participating countries. Ours is the restrictions on travel, forcing the introduction of what is to us an unknown substance into our bodies, they tell us it is to protect us.

Were we ever born free. We should remain free, an announcement on the mainstream news channel, by our then Prime Minister Boris Johnson, the main idiot in the plot. later he was to be removed, after being set up, for a fall. So, what is the simple plan? Step 1 create a worldwide disaster. Step 2 take away our identity by making us wear mask`s which also disguises our voice and shows us as a defeated subject. Whilst we are focusing on our fight to keep some dignity, lets engineer the return of the Taliban to Afghanistan, at this time who will care, when we are fighting for our own freedom.

How far did our government go to control us the people? Take the very people that are ment to defend us. The police. Use them to strike fear into the people they are ment to protect, the public.

Allow the leader of the Police force of our country, to say on television, words that encouraged the further division of people and gave the authority to break the law against stalking. How? By issuing a simple statement telling neighbours to watch and report any people who they thought maybe gathering together. In effect to commit the crime of stalking.

She was finally removed, when the police became excessively violent towards the already oppressed people, fighting for democracy, in our once United Kingdom. She was not as usual, held accountable for the fact that in her time in the job, a suspected predator, known by other officers collaborating with him. Was never reported on and their suspicions investigated immediately. The brotherhood protection, understandable and inevitable if the consequence of such protection is not punished severely. Those cowards protecting such an animal.

She was allowed to continue and assumably, still allowed to be paid her pension from the taxes paid by the people who she treated with contempt. Let her be given the minimal state pension.

Cooperation between the Leaders of the so-called free world to actually destroy people's freedom, is still at the forefront and although varies slightly between Countries, the laws to take away the very core of democracy and hence freedom of their people, appears still to be paramount.

Laws previously abhorred by the leaders of 'the free world.' Now are believed to be the only way to keep control of those people, using the methods previously condemned by these same hypocrites.

Keeping data is particularly important as you will see through this story, otherwise it would not have been possible to keep track of how bad is the manipulation we have all been subject too.

Although this story is about coming to terms and understanding the effects that my actions have had on me. Every person now has to come to terms with the devastating effects of our fragile freedom, one bat away from destruction. It is one of the same.

So back to my favourite subject. Me. I do not think I will ever be able to explain how I can predict other people's actions, just by the way they look or give off hidden signs. Accuse me of being bias against authority, but I have only ever found lies and deceit rife in authority. Even now I can see all the moves contriving to restrict us, way before they introduced them.

I did not see however, my wife's and my violation of our basic human rights under the Geneva convention coming. Of course, the Ombudsman, employed by the government, informed me there is around 14 months before it will be investigated to see if it was a violation. There must be an amazing number of human rights violations by the Government if it takes that long to investigate, we are now up to 13 Months.

Just to clarify.' The right to abode is set out in section 1(1) of the immigration act 1971 the foundation legislation for the current UK immigration law. The Home office puts it in another way in its guidance to officials, the right of abode is a 'complete exemption from UK immigration control. The right to 'live in, and to come and go into and from the United Kingdom without let and interference by the party in power.

Let us never forget, we have ALL lost our freedom for an increase of 0.01% of deaths (if true). This is a pandemic according to our government. Wouldn't it be simpler to shoot or gas those who try to travel or exercise their rights under the freedom of rights act and the magna carta? That may sound harsh, but let us not forget, many of the men sent to fight in both world wars, were forced to do so (Conscription), many under the threat of death by court martial if they refused to go happily to their death, what a choice. One day it could be yours.

Now our senior police, even, with the blessing of the government and our free press, encourage people to become stalkers and report people going against dreamt up rules, in themselves used to strike fear into vulnerable people.

Harass the public with numbers of Deaths within 28days of a positive test, why? Then to try to get workers back to work the need to isolate, was officially reduced to only 10 days then further reduced to 8 days of isolation?

Rules made up for the police to put fear into people, to ensure they limited exercise for no proven benefit, and in the end allowed murder to be easily committed on the vulnerable section of our community, young girls. With no fitting punishment, for the perpetrator or those that suspected him and by that allowed it to happen.

Where are our protectors? The politicians WE voted for, the police WE pay for, the army WE pay for, the judges WE pay for. Where were they all? How is what they have done to our beloved democracy been achievable?

The simple answer, known and understood by all State controlled leaders, FEAR AND DIVISION = CONTROL OF THE MASSES.

But in our case this fear is only temporary they claim, as it is only to protect us from a pandemic, a pandemic up to March 2021 claiming 125,000 deaths, in other words, even assuming this figure to be true. Around 0.19%, 2019 it was 0.18%.

True democracy requires dissemination of too much knowledge, in an understandable and coherent manner to reach all people. We do not have anyone capable of that, the so-called experts, handpicked for their limited knowledge on the precise subject coupled with a bunch of bumbling idiots, more interested in breaking their own rules, partying, and squeezing women's arses, in the name of falling in love, according to the announcement of one such, still serving MP appearing in a popular TV game show, paying him a considerable amount of money, on top of his incom paid from our taxes.

How much simpler then, to remove the freedom of speech and movement. Introduce so called emergency rules, at any time to control its people. We find that members of the conservative government have been given honour's for destroying our economy and violating our civil rights, is this now the normal or just a move to get more conservatives into the house of Lords?

Why don't the people, rich, poor and those in the middle, join, to demand the explanations of why both our major parties want to 'set person against person to destroy our dignity' (Winston Churchill quotation).

Just like parents with their children, how easy it is for governments, to take away the freedom of their people.

The very fact that our country is classed as a democratic and free one, has given us the security of mind, that we are not controlled by a regime. Similar to the ones our older generation fought against, like the NAZI REGIME. The regime hell bent on bringing everyone worldwide under control and destroying everyone who opposed their methods.

The Nazi party used fear, not only directed towards other races of people, but their own people also, who disagreed with their methods of control.

How is this relevant to my story? Simple all lives are, affected, when the need for a government or even parent, to fully explain and be accountable for their actions is ignored. Removal of long-established laws and protections, because of a temporary situation, not even adequately defined or qualified as a national emergency, but designed simply to generate fear by the minority, into the majority.

Was this even put to a vote by, the total numbers with the required expert knowledge, to collectively decide on the life changing actions to be taken by a government, devoid of the required knowledge to make such a life changing action? No.

Only the few pre-designated 'experts' who already knew what the required outcome was going to be, the outcome their paymasters needed.

Along with the parties standing for the views of the other voters. They didn`t count because there wasn`t the need to have a vote on the peoples view on this so defined Pandemic. Just to make sure divide and conquer. Split the people and divide the country, give an idea that the people have control, divide England, Ireland, Scotland, and Wales. Give their leaders the required preconceived actions but allow slight variations to give the appearance of disagreements between the peoples of the UNITED

KINGDOM. Divide and conquer! Classic and effective.

Just the presence of so-called experts, paid as advisors to the Government in power and promised titles. Were to confuse and frighten as many of the masses as possible.

The added factor was to put alongside these experts, responsible politicians. Some more interested in flaunting the fact they could break their own rules, and still remain a politician, using his or her status to extract more money. Why? Because their portrayal, is as experts in a specific jobs and positions. Bullshit, they are just workers, used by the governments to generate fear in the masses, and told the direction the advice must take, for a price of course.

Definition of these experts. (Knows everything in his or her field). Modification of the word expert, in this period of time, EX-SPURT. (Over the hill little drip).

Actions put in place by people who, in the end, disappear from the scene. Never to be proven to be incompetent in their related actions and re-actions, decorated and then disappear, avoiding any retributions. Remember them?

The greatest fear we should have, is the ignoring of all common laws of the land, introduction of monetary fines designed to destroy the freedom of the poorer majority and those less sure of our rights under common law. This along with no free access to legal redress of the incompetence of the perpetrators.

If this is not bad enough, these bunch of 'normal' people (politicians), were given the rights to govern, because of the votes of the people, on the understanding they follow the existing laws of our Country and protect the rights to our freedoms. This never happened, yet no one is held to account, in fact they are promoted to their level of incompetence, by more senior incompetents, with the assurance that when they are indeed exposed as incompetent, they can return to their earlier job, at which many were originally incompetent anyway. Wow lots of use of the word Incompetence.

Where was our Beloved Queen (she had no power), our Lords (they had no power), Judges (they had no power), lawyers (no power), Real competent local politicians (non-existent), Police, the very people who should be protecting our civil rights? Suppressed, controlled, overruled by bullies in their own ranks.

All of the above, further divided by allowing different rules for divided countries within our small Island, for their own progression to gain more power. Unfortunately, by the very fact our country is known as democratic, this means further division caused by patriotism for the sake of opposing the main Government, even though these patriots are being paid by the same Government. Confusing? That's the way its planned.

Who have allowed these appointed figureheads, to gain power to suppress people to a greater extent than ever before? Further dividing the people of the once United Kingdom? We all have.

Lack of unity, allowing maximum division, greater confusion of the people. Aim at a 48:52% split, on how the various decisions, including the political party, in term are made.

In fact, this split is assuming everyone takes part in a vote. Usually that is not the case, sometimes, depending upon the topic, the percentage of those voting will be only 60% of those qualifying. This over the recent years has reduced the number of political parties, capable of challenging the competence of the two main parties, whose mercy we are now at.

Their actions so far being the proven method leading to control of the masses. One of introducing FEAR, CHAOS, DEVESTATION and DESPARE into our lives.

As we now know, a referendum is granted, only when the political party in power believes the people will give them the upper hand. This time the so-called Brexit referendum was perfectly planned to coincide with the need to reset the meaning of democracy. How is it possible that now the so called COVID 19 is identified as a new strain to FLU, bullshit again, when both are of the same basic strain of coronavirus-sars2. Discovered in the middle East, found in a mammal, in the 17th century.

Chapter 32

Where are the bats now?

So how can so much fear be created from bats. Were we all controlled, and many allowed to die in isolation from their loved ones, just to appease the people who adore bats? Of course, not this would be entirely ridiculous. So once again we all were fed Bullshit, or in this case Batshit. Just to create a pandemic. A word I doubt very few knew the significance of. Epidemic would not have given the world stage to the World leaders. Let's not forget they were ALL united!

So, unless, bats had suddenly been stopped from flying out of their caves (we could have called that 'locked down' had they been human). This explanation sounds like the usual rubbish we are used to.

So why was world travel stopped, for all but the rich and famous? Nothing made, or makes any sense, other than to see if the people can be divided and controlled by their fear of death, over common sense. If that's case, then well-done World leaders 'theory proven'.

We all need the same basic things to survive, but some will never even get to the beginning of adult life. It is all a game of chance, including how where and when we are borne and die. Although I do not even profess to have read the bible to any depth, one saying I remember is 'to live you only have to die.' this simple quotation could say it all, your last point of living will be your last memory, which of course you couldn't recall. Unless you do live past the point of death in some way.

Maybe there are parallel layers (zones), in what we call time, and each layer can be accessed, simply because a solid body is not needed to send pure data, only electronic pulses. So, what if, at the instant of release from the solid body. There is movement from one zone to another in blocks of pure data.

Then a data collection host accepts this. A body in another time zone., or evolutionary period, maybe.

It has always been intriguing, how our rapid progression made in the understanding of science accelerates with each generation? Maybe we could consider that complete revolutions of time periods happen, I call them time zones as above.

Within that time zone knowledge becomes stored, the next period begins with the blocks of stored knowledge transmitted to the new human forms born (collection hosts). Therefore, the beginning of the next time zone, generation, or period. More than one set of knowledge is now existing within the new life. So, this period of existence begins with all the knowledge from both zones.

As everything is, encased in an atmosphere surrounded by a void, time zones themselves then carry-on building from an enhanced state and at ever increasing speed.

Then as long as the planet itself survives, each time zone storing a greater amount of data, grows ever more. Then finally the planet can no longer produce the materials to advance the knowledge of the possible sciences. If in the period up to this point no other source is found to supply what is necessary for progression. Everything dies and it all begins again.

Has this creation already happened, is this why sometimes we feel like we know what is going to happen before it does? Why all of a sudden are we told we must preserve the continuation of this planet at any cost? Preservation is not enough; transformation is the only answer.

We already find links from literature or science produced, way before proof of the science has been recognised.

At present we cannot positively link the present to the future, only the present to the past. A simple example is the book 1984. In 1984 if we had understood it to be a fairly true prediction of what was to happen in the then future. Maybe could have done certain things to accelerate our understanding of life and slow down our route to self-destruction. but we never seem to learn to accept the predictions from those links to the past, until it is too late to be effective.

The real question I and many others of advancing age ask is, what is it like to be really old? Because age appears to limit the power of understanding developments in advanced technology at best, and for me that`s sad.

I do not feel any different, than when I was that youth gaining life experiences. Even now I have to try to control that same rage inside me, but no longer have the energy, to do that successfully, even my empathy has almost gone.

Our children, now adults, don't really have the time to understand what it is like, because outwardly we have accepted the changes, all be it at different speeds. They are now just a younger version of us oldies, but still with hope and in possession of ever-increasing conflicting explanations of happenings in the past. They now have a title, conspiracy theories.

I despair, as I watch the antics of governments and so-called World leaders, Look at our tiny country. Five different prime ministers in less than a term of office Four of them with no input from the United Kingdom voters. The first one resigned because the voters, voted for what they thought best for our country, with the limited understandable information we were all given.

He was the one, unable to give a convincing argument as to why his view was correct. So, he threw his dummy out of the pram and abandoned his duties, appearing at Wimbledon tennis, just to rub in the status, afforded to a failure with contempt for the People of the United Kingdom.

The second PM voted in by inept children recruited as conservative members to make up the numbers needed to vote in someone to conduct an almost impossible task, get a good deal on leaving the EU.

Committed all of a sudden to following the small majority of voters' wishes, Impossible. Then she had to go, let us try someone else. But he became dangerous and set the rules to destroy our democracy. They called it a pandemic. BULLSHIT it was and still is a test to gauge the ability to control the people by fear.

The only thing I will say in his favour, he outwardly showed in his bumbling way, that he didn`t believe the bullshit he was forced to come out with. He was forced to show unity with the rest of the so-called free world bullshitters. He was having the problem of following the rules he had to set.

Wheel in the inept children again. A new Prime minister, the best of the bunch. A fantastic strategist, a strong woman to take on the worst economic situation in many years.

No, the shortest term served by a prime minister

ever, just weeks. Need we panic? Answer no wheel in the children, lets vote in one of the losers from the last disastrous vote, but it has to be someone unique. Yes, tell the children to vote for the rich failure, he is different, his wife is a millionaire as well, they will not need to have dodgy loans and he is always grinning no matter how bad the announcement. How true that is.

Don't let him mess up, we might have to hand control over to the other bunch that did everything to destroy democracy like us but got away with it by conforming. Thank God for the old labour party and our friends the G20.

The Guardian Paper claims to have spent the past years tirelessly investigating the shortcomings of the Tories in office – austerity, Brexit, party gate, cronyism, the Truss debacle, and the individual failings of ministers who behave as if the rules don't apply to them.

This has resulted in resignations, apologies, and policy corrections, revelations about Nadhim Zahawi and Dominic Raab are just the latest in a lengthy line of important scoops. And with an election just round the corner, it's crucial that we can all make informed decisions about who is best to lead the UK. Reporting is vital for democracy, for fairness and to demand better from the powerful.

Let us never be directly and indirectly threatening with fines, imprisonment, isolation and even death, to reset the world climate. More importantly how long before the so-called temporary measures to cope with a non-existent Pandemic be continuously brought back?

All this uncertainty and panic, caused by some bats and peasants in a live animal market. The saying of you can fool some of the people all the time, all the people some of the time, but you can`t fool all the people all the time, had to be quantified. Of course, the so-called free world's governments were too unified in their approach to control the masses, to ever consider what was best for their individual people.

We can still save face for another year; we tried spending a fortune on technological advances that are actually regressive. Like billions of pounds to develop a serum to divide the world and prevent travel.

That worked and the added bonus, it frightened the old and infirm, even their children let them die alone. Now that's control.

So, to all you yet to be born, if you do find this book somewhere in the distant future, alter the parts that make no obvious sense in this concluding chapter, (probably the zoning), and leave it in a place where it can easily be found. If we are part of an ever revolving, unending universal orbit, then. Get it out into the media so we might all read and understand what's going to happen next.

To Jackie, see you again, in the light house, wearing the green Mackintosh. Give me a smile I might even remember you; If I do, we can save some time.

To Our Children, next time around, give us a break, we had to learn too, even now we do not know everything, but we might know more than you think.

And remember. You can't always get what you want, but if you try some time, you just might find you can get what you need.

Thanks to my past and everyone that's been in it, even you, Father. Remember I could have been the perfect SON you never understood, but I never knew how to make it right.

BON VOYAGE TO EVERYONE, HERE'S TO MEETING AGAIN IN A BETTER PLACE AND WITH GREATER UNDERSTANDING OF WHAT LIFE CAN BE.